The Digital Marketplace Navigating the World of E-Commerce

Johnathan Reynolds

Copyright © [2023]

Author: Johnathan Reynolds

Title: The Digital Marketplace Navigating the World of E-Commerce

All rights reserved. No part of this book may be reproduced or transmitted in any form or by any means, electronic or mechanical, including photocopying, recording, or by any information storage and retrieval system, without permission in writing from the author.

This book is a product of

ISBN:

Table of content

Chapter name	Page No
1. The Rise of Online Shopping	1
2. Creating a Virtual Storefront	32
3. Strategies for Online Stores	60
4. Establishing a Powerful Online Identity	68
5. Marketing Methods in the Digital Age	80
6. Interaction With Users And The Customer Experience	101
7. Security and Settlements	118
8. Controlling Stock and Meeting Orders	134
9. Decision Making Through Analysing Data	149
10. Online Shopping's Bright Future	162

Chapter 1:
The Rise of Online Shopping

1.1- Historical context of e-commerce.

Introduction

The business world has changed dramatically during the past few decades. The development of the internet and other digital technologies opened up a new market where goods and services could be bought and sold regardless of location. Because of this development, the term "e-commerce," which stands for "electronic commerce," has entered the common lexicon. However, the road to modern e-commerce begins long before the dot-com boom. The significance of e-commerce in the modern world can only be grasped by looking back at its origins, growth, and change over time.

Introduction: The Beginnings of Electronic Commerce

First Commercial Activities, Section 1.1

Commercial exchange predates modern human civilisation. Humans have long been looking for ways to trade value, from bargaining for products and services in early marketplaces through the development of market towns. These earlier modes of trade paved the way for the modern online marketplace.

Financial and Banking Instruments Evolved in Section 1.2

Trade practises shifted as societies developed. The introduction of coinage in ancient Lydia and the growth of banking in ancient Greece and Rome were both pivotal moments in the history of trade. These developments paved the way for the contemporary monetary system by making transactions easier.

Explorers and merchants of the world, rejoice!

A new era of trade began in the 15th and 16th centuries, when Europeans set out to find new sea routes and grow their empires. Early antecedents to global trade included the Silk Road, which linked Asia and Europe, and the spice trade, which travelled from the East Indies to Europe.

1.4% The Beginning of the Industrial Age

The Industrial Revolution occurred in the 18th and 19th centuries, and it was a time of great technological innovation that altered the production and distribution of products. The advent of steam power, railroads, and telegraph networks ushered in the modern business era.

Chapter 2: Electronic Data Interchange

2.10 Catalogues Sent in the Mail

Mail-order catalogues, one of the earliest types of remote shopping, emerged in the 19th century. In the United States, mail-order merchants such as Sears, Roebuck and Co. and Montgomery Ward gave customers a large selection of goods.

2.2 Early Communication Networks, Including the Telegraph

Long-distance communication took a giant step forward with the invention of the telegraph in the middle of the 19th century. Businesses were able to send orders and data more quickly, which sped up logistics and commercial operations. Telegraph systems were a precursor to the modern communication technologies that underpin electronic commerce.

EDI (Electronic Data Interchange) was born in 2.3.

EDI, or electronic data interchange, first appeared in the middle of the twentieth century. Electronic data interchange (EDI) systems made it possible for companies to electronically exchange structured data for the purposes of inventory and order processing. While electronic data interchange (EDI) is not the same thing as modern e-commerce, it did pave the way for the digital exchange of information that underpins it.

The Internet and Its Impact on Society (Chapter 3)
3.1.1 The Birth of the Internet

The Internet, a worldwide system of linked computers, appeared as a transformative force in the second half of the twentieth century. In the 1990s, the internet was made available to the general public after having been developed for military and academic use. This had a profound impact on the commercial landscape.

The Internet and Message Boards (MBSs) 3.2.1

CompuServe and Prodigy were two of the earliest online services that allowed for online commerce and conversation before the advent of the World Wide Web. BBSs paved the way for the development of the online communities that would fuel e-commerce with its message boards and classified ads.

The First Electronic Commerce Transactions and the Development of the World Wide Web 3.3

In 1991, Tim Berners-Lee unveiled what would become known as the World Wide Web. It enabled the production of hypertext documents viewable in web browsers. This innovation ushered in the modern era of the internet and paved the way for the growth of e-commerce as we know it today.

Books.com, the Original Virtual Bookstore 3.4

The American Booksellers Association was one of the earliest internet commerce pioneers, launching "Books.com" in 1992. Online book shopping was made possible by this service, paving the way for the countless markets that followed.

Chapter 4: The Plunge and Recovery of the Dot-Com Industry

4.1.1 The Internet Boom

The IT sector experienced unprecedented development and speculation during the infamous dot-com boom of the late 1990s. Startups that claimed to transform the way we shop received billions of dollars in funding, and e-commerce giants led the way.

4.2 Amazon and eBay, Early Leaders in Online Shopping

Amazon and eBay were two of the most prominent dot-com firms of the late 1990s and early 2000s. Jeff Bezos established Amazon in 1994 as an online bookshop, but it has now grown into a full-fledged marketplace. Pierre Omidyar launched eBay in 1995 as a website where users could buy and sell products online through auctions.

4.3 The Plunge of the Internet Economy

The early 2000s saw the end of the dot-com bubble and the euphoria that came with it. Even after receiving large financing, many e-commerce firms ended up failing or filing for bankruptcy. A major market downturn occurred as investors saw that online retail profits were not a given.

The Consolidation of the Market and the Rise of the E-Commerce Giants

5.1 The Rise of Amazon

Amazon persevered through the dot-com bust by growing and diversifying even as its competitors failed. It evolved from a virtual bookstore into a place to buy virtually anything. Foreshadowing its future domination in the e-commerce sector, Amazon's success proved the enormous potential of online retail.

eBay and the Emergence of Electronic Markets, Section 5.2

eBay established itself as a frontrunner in the e-commerce industry by creating the concept of online auctions and marketplaces. It opened up a new market for online shopping by facilitating the sale and purchase of items between private parties. In the future, the gig economy and online markets would also benefit from this groundbreaking concept.

Expanding Globally: Alibaba in 5.

Alibaba was started by Jack Ma in 1999, and since then it has grown to become a dominant player in both the Chinese and global e-commerce marketplaces. Alibaba's success demonstrated the worldwide potential of online shopping and the significance of adjusting to various consumer bases.

Mergers and Acquisitions in the Market

Large firms continued their trend of market consolidation via mergers and acquisitions as they realised the significance of e-commerce in the modern era. Traditional brick-and-mortar retailers like Walmart, for instance, have undertaken strategic investments and acquisitions to strengthen their online presence and compete with Amazon.

Chapter 6: The Developments in Technology and New Methods of Making Payments

Safe Payment Processors 6.1

The development of new technologies has been crucial to the expansion of online shopping. Encryption methods and the widespread use of secure payment gateways have made internet shopping a more secure and more convenient option. Consumers' greater faith in the safety of their financial data translated to more purchases being made online.

Mobile commerce (6.2)

M-commerce)

Mobile devices, especially smartphones, have facilitated a dramatic shift in the e-commerce landscape. Consumers' ability to purchase while on the road was a major factor in the expansion of the e-commerce market. Companies now have to consider mobile devices when developing their online stores.

Payment Options, Section 6.3

Alternative payment methods have gained popularity, despite the continued use of credit and debit cards. PayPal, Apple Pay, and Google Pay are all digital wallets that may be used to make online transactions. Bitcoin and other cryptocurrencies have gained traction in online business because they provide anonymous, cross-border trade.

A.6. BNPL Services (Buy Now, Pay Later)

Customers' habits regarding making purchases on the internet have shifted since the introduction of buy now, pay later (BNPL) services.

With BNPL systems like Afterpay and Klarna, customers may divide the cost of a large purchase into manageable monthly payments. This method of payment has recently acquired traction among younger consumers, which has led to its adoption by online marketplaces.

The Effects of Globalisation on Electronic Commerce

7.1.1 International online trade

The advent of e-commerce has removed physical barriers, allowing companies to sell to consumers all over the globe. Small businesses and startups now have a chance to reach customers all over the world thanks to the proliferation of e-commerce. Shopify and Etsy have made it possible for anyone to open their own online shop and sell to customers all around the world.

Global Markets and Business Competition

Increased competitiveness among companies is another effect of cross-border e-commerce. To succeed in today's global economy, businesses must respond to shifting customer demands, comply with ever-changing trade restrictions, and continually improve their offerings. As a result, several sectors have been able to innovate and specialise.

Influencer marketing and social media platforms, chapter 8.

The Influence of Social Media on Online Shopping 8.1

To conduct business online, social media sites are now necessities. Many companies today use social media to communicate with their consumers, promote new goods, and reach certain demographics. Social media sites like Facebook, Instagram, and Pinterest have made it easier for users to make purchases by incorporating tools like "Shop Now" buttons and shoppable posts.

8.2 The Impact of Influencer Marketing

For online retailers, influencer marketing has become an increasingly effective strategy. Sales are typically significantly impacted when social media influencers with huge audiences endorse products and services to their followers. The way in which brands interact with their target audiences and pique their attention has been revolutionised by this type of advertising.

User-created content (also known as UGC) 8.3

Customer evaluations and other forms of user-generated material have become increasingly valuable to online retailers. Consumers place a high value on the insights and feedback of their peers when out shopping. Online stores promote and display UGC as a means of increasing customer confidence in their brand.

Chapter 9: The Development of Financial Transactions

9.1 New Developments in Recurring Payments

Along with the rise of e-commerce, new payment mechanisms have emerged. Contactless payments, biometric authentication, and voice-activated transactions are just some of the ongoing advancements while traditional card payments remain popular. These innovations are made to strengthen safety and simplify the purchasing procedure.

9.2 Emerging Markets and Financial Inclusion

By making global online marketplaces more accessible to those living in developing countries, e-commerce has helped expand people's access to financial services. People in areas without easy access to conventional banking systems can now engage in e-commerce thanks to the proliferation of mobile banking and payment services.

Chapter 10: "Online Business and the COVID-19 Outbreak"

The Pandemic and the Explosion of Online Shopping

The 2019 COVID-19 epidemic hit late and hit e-commerce hard. Many conventional stores had to temporarily seal their doors as a result of lockdowns and other forms of social separation. In light of this, many people have started doing their shopping online instead.

10.2 Continued Expansion and Shifting Consumer Habits

E-commerce has continued to expand even as regulations have loosened because many consumers prefer the convenience of shopping from home. Consumers have shifted their shopping patterns to include more diverse online purchases, such as food and home office supplies. The retail industry's transition to digital was hastened by this change.

10.3 Opportunities and Threats

Businesses faced difficulties as a result of the pandemic, but they also had possibilities. E-commerce businesses changed to match the rising demand, and conventional stores sped up their digital initiatives. As a result of the pandemic, new innovations in contactless delivery, curbside pickup, and digital shopping experiences arose.

Chapter Eleven: What's Next for Online Shopping

11.1 Ongoing Improvements in Technology

We can expect e-commerce to undergo further changes in the future. The future of this industry is being shaped by a number of trends and developments, including:

There will be an increase in the use of AI-powered personalised shopping experiences, chatbots for customer service, and cutting-edge recommendation systems.

- Augmented Reality (AR) and Virtual Reality (VR): Consumers will be able to virtually try on apparel, see products in their own homes, and have a better online shopping experience as a result of these technologies.

More and more shoppers are thinking twice about how their choices may affect the planet. In response, the e-commerce industry is implementing eco-friendly policies including carbon-neutral shipping and environmentally-friendly packaging.

- Omnichannel Retail: As companies invest in omnichannel strategy, the line between online and offline retail will continue to blur, enabling customers to easily transition between digital and physical shopping.

Globalisation will continue, and e-commerce that spans national boundaries will become easier for small and medium-sized enterprises to implement, boosting international trade.

11.2 Online Trade in Developing Economies

Expanding internet availability and rising consumer incomes give opportunities for firms in emerging economies, which will contribute to the expansion of e-commerce into these regions. Success in these areas will depend heavily on mobile-first initiatives and localised approaches.

11.3, Ethical and Regulatory Considerations

The likes of data privacy, cybersecurity, and competition will be scrutinised more closely in the future of e-commerce. Antitrust issues and consumer protection are two areas that governments and regulatory agencies will work to improve in the future of the industry.

Conclusion

The development of trade from its earliest stages to the modern online marketplace provides an interesting backdrop to the history of e-commerce. To fully appreciate the present significance of e-commerce, it is crucial to first understand its origins. Even while the landscape of e-commerce is always shifting, one thing is certain: this revolutionary force will forever alter the ways in which we shop, do business, and communicate with one another and the rest of the world. The evolution of e-commerce is more than simply a fascinating tale; it also provides valuable insights into the future of business.

1.2- The impact of e-commerce on traditional retail.

Introduction

The retail sector, vital to the functioning of the global economy, has seen profound change in the last few decades. The proliferation of online business is largely responsible for this shift. E-commerce, or the exchange of products and services through the internet, has emerged as a dominant force in the retail industry in recent decades. Traditional retail, such as malls and long-standing stores, has been profoundly affected by the rise of e-commerce, and this offers several causes for concern. We will look at how e-commerce has changed customer habits, impacted brick-and-mortar stores, and forced established merchants to adjust to a new and dynamic competitive field.

The Origins of Retail and Business Chapter 1

1.1 The Importance of Trade Throughout History

Trading has been practised by humans since their earliest civilizations. Trading products and services has been an integral element of human life for centuries. Cultures, economics, and civilizations have all been influenced by commerce, from the first marketplaces in Mesopotamia to the modern Silk Road.

The Beginning of Retail 1.2

In ancient marketplaces and bazaars, retail as a distinct idea first emerged. The term "retail" describes the practise of selling wares to end users in very small amounts. Historically, retailing progressed from unstructured barter systems to more formalised forms of trade, such as monetary exchanges.

The Importance of Brick-and-Mortar Shops

In the history of trade, the advent of brick-and-mortar stores is a watershed moment. Having a specific location in which to view and evaluate a variety of products before making a purchase was made possible by the existence of stores. A new era of materialism was ushered in with the advent of malls and shopping centres.

Section 2: 20th Century Brick-and-Mortar Retail

Increase in Department Stores, Section 2.1

The 20th century saw the rise of massive shopping malls and department stores like Macy's and Harrods. These gigantic, multi-level stores brought a new dimension to the shopping experience by housing a dizzying array of goods in a single location. For shoppers in search of both variety and convenience, department stores quickly became household names.

2.2.1 The Growth of Shopping Centres
In the middle of the twentieth century, enclosed shopping malls with climate control became a fixture of the suburbs of the United States. Shopping malls consolidated a wide variety of businesses into a single location, making it convenient for families to do all of their shopping and visiting one place.

Big-Box Superstores and Their Market Dominance 2.3

In the second part of the twentieth century, big-box stores like Walmart and Target rose to popularity. Large-format retailers like these catered to price-conscious shoppers by stocking a wide variety of goods at low prices. They were able to achieve this level of retail dominance thanks to their large physical presence and well-oiled supply chains.

Third Chapter: The Birth of Electronic Commerce

Changes Caused by the Internet (3.1)

The internet, a worldwide system of linked computers, emerged in the late 20th century. This technological advancement paved the way for the digitalization of business. The internet was created for government and academic use, but it was soon opened up to the public, paving the way for online shopping.

3.2.1 The Growth of E-Commerce

With the advent of reliable online payment systems in the early 1990s, internet shopping quickly gained popularity. Buying things through online marketplaces was a revolutionary concept that changed the way people shopped forever.

Dot-com times, 3.3.1

The "dot-com" era flourished in the late 1990s and early 2000s, a time marked by the meteoric rise of new businesses built on the internet. E-commerce was a primary emphasis for many of these new businesses, which hoped to profit from the expanding online marketplace. The dot-com bubble crash took down some companies, while others went on to become household names.

Part Four: The Revolution Against Mainstream Retail

4.1 Evolving Purchase Patterns

Online shopping's widespread availability and ease of use began to influence shoppers' habits. Consumers appreciated the convenience of being able to shop, check out and pay for items without leaving the house. The effects of this change in consumer behaviour on brick-and-mortar establishments were significant.

4.2 Retailer Vacancies and Store Closures

Store closures and retail vacancies are direct results of the fall in foot traffic. Once-prominent shopping malls and department stores struggled to keep up with the times as retailing evolved. Job losses and the alteration of city and suburbiascapes were just two of the economic and social effects of these closures.

Retail Chapter 4.3 Failures

Due to financial difficulties, some conventional stores have declared bankruptcy. The difficulties presented by e-commerce rivalry and shifting consumer tastes were highlighted by the failures of brick-and-mortar retailers like Toys "R" Us and Sears.

Loss of Market Share, Section 4.4

Traditional merchants saw a rapid expansion of competition from e-commerce giants like Amazon. Amazon's extensive product catalogue, low prices, and streamlined shipping and delivery systems made it a serious rival.

Chapter 5: The Changing Nature of Online Shoppers

An Important Motivating Factor: 5.1 Convenience

The ease of online shopping is a major factor in its widespread popularity. Online retailers now offer round-the-clock service, a plethora of goods, and home delivery to their customers. Consumers' expectations have been modified as a result of this added ease.

5.2 Shopping Around

Online marketplaces make price comparisons much easier. The consumer market has made it simple to investigate products, get feedback from others, and compare pricing from various vendors. Because of this openness, customers are able to make well-informed purchasing judgements.

5.3.1 Customization and Suggestions

Data analytics and AI-driven algorithms are used by e-commerce platforms to personalise the buying experience for each individual user. Better conversion rates can be achieved through e-commerce when product suggestions are made based on previous browsing and buying behaviour.

The Importance of Feedback and Rankings

E-commerce would not be what it is today without customer reviews and feedback. Consumers trust the opinions of other consumers as a gauge of product quality and reliability. In the same way that rave evaluations can increase business, scathing ones can drive customers away.

Chapter 6: The Fall of Brick-and-Mortar Shops

6.1 Retailer Vacancies and Store Closures

There has been a dramatic shift away from brick-and-mortar retailers. Malls and retail areas that used to be booming are now having trouble because fewer people go shopping there. Many neighbourhoods and suburbs now feature an abundance of empty stores.

Showrooming and Webrooming, Section 6.2

The introduction of electronic commerce prompted a shift in consumer habits. Consumers' practise of "showrooming," in which they visit brick-and-mortar establishments to try out things before buying them online for a lower price, has grown in popularity. Instead of physically going to a store to make a purchase, some people prefer to do their research online beforehand.

The Merging of Digital and Physical Worlds 6.3

Some established stores have seen the need to bridge the gap between online and physical purchasing. Omnichannel retailing makes it easy for customers to make purchases via any available channel, be it online or in a store. The gap between online and in-store buying is closed through services like buy online, pick up in-store (BOPIS).

6.4 Retailer Enhancements and Novelties

Some brick-and-mortar stores, realising they needed to adapt or die, prioritised increasing the in-store buying experience. Retailers have put time and money on in-store design, interactive displays, and immersive technologies to compete with the convenience of online buying.

Chapter Seven: The Emergence of Online Aggregators and Markets

7.1 The Prevalence of Electronic Markets

Amazon and other online marketplaces

online marketplaces, with Amazon, eBay, and Alibaba rising to prominence. These marketplaces provide customers with easy access to several vendors and their wares. However, their monopoly status has prompted antitrust and competition worries.

Intensified Rivalry 7.2

Traditional shops face heightened levels of competition due to the rise of online marketplaces. The low prices and easy accessibility of these platforms make it difficult for smaller firms to compete. The difficulty lies in setting themselves out from the competition and fostering customer loyalty.

Seller Difficulties 7.3

Online marketplaces offer a way for businesses to access a large number of customers, but they also present some difficulties. It's not easy being a seller in today's market, what with all the fees, rivalry, and potential loss of influence over consumer perception and interaction.

Innovations in Technology and the Supply Chain

8.1 Warehouses and Distribution Centres

Companies like Amazon, which dominates the online retail market, have spent billions on warehouses and fulfilment centres. These distribution centres are placed strategically to facilitate quick order processing and dependable transport. The growth of online shopping can largely be attributed to the improvements in logistics and storage that have been made.

8.2 Finish-Line Distribution Options

There has been a lot of attention paid to the "last mile" of delivery, or the final stretch from the warehouse to the consumer's front door. Businesses are looking into ways to speed up last-mile deliveries by experimenting with drones, driverless cars, and crowdsourcing.

Managing stock and analysing data: Section 8.3
Modern data analytics and inventory management solutions are vital to the success of online retailers. The necessity for products to be immediately available is balanced by the aim to minimise surplus inventory, which can be costly for retailers. Pricing, stock levels, and

advertising approaches can all be improved with the use of data and AI-driven tools.

Chapter 9: Traditional Retail's Survival Strategy

Strategies for Omnichannel Retailing 9.1

As they see how online and physical channels can work together, many brick-and-mortar stores have adopted omnichannel strategy. It is now crucial for businesses to provide services like BOPIS, curbside pickup, and seamless online-to-offline interactions in order to thrive.

9.2 Improved Shopper Interactions

There are certain brick-and-mortar retailers that have made it a priority to improve the in-store encounter. They attract customers who care about more than just expediency by providing a pleasant environment, attractive product displays, and individualised service.

9.3 Customer Loyalty and Participation

The use of client loyalty programmes has increased in recent years. To encourage repeat business and improve client connections, conventional merchants provide prizes, discounts, and special privileges.

Joint Efforts and Partnerships 9.4

Traditional retailers have expanded their reach and capacities through partnerships with e-commerce platforms, delivery services, and related industries. By working together, they may leverage the benefits of the digital environment.

9.5 Niche and localised

Some stores have done well by targeting specific clientele or by putting an emphasis on their regional prominence and ties to the surrounding area. They can attract devoted customers by standing out from the competition with novel goods and services.

Chapter 10: What's Next for Brick-and-Mortar Stores

10.2 Ongoing Creativity and Technological Advancement

If they want to survive, brick-and-mortar stores will need to innovate and embrace new technologies. Money is being put into supply chain optimisation, data analytics, and internet sales platforms. The value of AI-driven solutions for customization and user engagement will rise over time.

In 10.2 Sustainability and Social Responsibility

The general public's consciousness of ecological and social concerns is elevating. Sustainable and socially-responsible practises at conventional stores can win over environmentally-conscious shoppers and set them apart from competitors.

Business models that can change with the times (10.3)

It is essential that company concepts be adaptable. Retailers need to be flexible and open to new strategies as the market and customer tastes evolve. Maintaining competitiveness will necessitate adopting agile tactics.

10.4 Localization and Community Involvement

For brick-and-mortar stores, nothing is more important than their standing in the community. Local commerce may thrive with the help of active and devoted communities.

Chapter Eleven: "Conclusion: Mapping the Future of E-Commerce"

11.1 The Coexistence of Electronic Commerce and Brick-and-Mortar Stores

The future of retail will be determined by how well online shopping and brick-and-mortar stores can coexist. Retailers who can anticipate their customers' changing wants and needs, make good use of available technologies, and design compelling, one-of-a-kind experiences to bridge the gap between online and in-store purchasing will thrive.

11.2 The Lasting Effect of E-Commerce

Online shopping has had a huge and lasting effect on brick-and-mortar stores. It has changed the way people shop, posing serious challenges to conventional merchants who have not yet adapted to the new shopping landscape. Traditional retail, however, has room to grow and prosper in a world where e-commerce is shaping the future of business.

Epilogue

The influence of online shopping on brick-and-mortar stores is one of reinvention and creativity. It's a story that exemplifies the retail sector's adaptability and flexibility in the face of shifting consumer tastes and technology developments. The future of shopping, business, and global trade is inextricably intertwined with the existence of both online and brick-and-mortar retail. The constant difficulty for brick-and-mortar and online stores alike in this dynamic marketplace is adapting to the changing preferences of customers.

1.3- Evolution of online shopping.

Introduction

Online shopping's meteoric rise exemplifies how far technology has come in its ability to revolutionise business and buyer habits. What started as a revolutionary idea only a few decades ago has become a global industry that has changed the way people all over the world buy and sell products and services. This in-depth look will travel over the many years of internet shopping's development, from its infancy to the present day. Along the way, we'll take a look at the ways in which e-commerce has influenced business, economics, and cultures around the world, including the rise of new technologies and the evolution of consumer tastes.

The Beginning of Electronic Commerce

1.1 Early Examples of Digital Trade

Online purchasing has been around since the early days of the internet. Some forward-thinking people in the 1970s and 1980s, when computer networks were only taking shape, imagined doing business online. Online bulletin board systems and primitive electronic payment techniques were among the earliest forms of digital business.

1.2 New and Original Ideas
Several ground-breaking ideas developed in the late 1980s and early 1990s formed the basis for today's ubiquitous online purchasing. One of the most important was the concept of encrypted payment systems, which allowed for safe online transactions. Early online markets like CompuServe's Electronic Mall showed consumers the potential benefits of online buying.

1.3 The Original Online Stores

The first internet stores opened their virtual doors in the 1990s. In 1994, Jeff Bezos started an online bookshop called Amazon.com, which eventually grew into a retail juggernaut. Just a year later, Pierre Omidyar created eBay, an online marketplace where users could conduct auction-style purchases and sales. These forerunner businesses proved the viability of e-commerce and got people used to the idea of buying things without leaving their houses.

Section 2: The Internet Bubble and Plunge

Dot-com fever (2.1)

The term "dot-com boom" refers to the period of time in the late 1990s when a lot of money was being gambled on internet-related firms. Companies that facilitate online purchasing saw a significant increase in both interest and funding. E-commerce sites have mushroomed as a result of the rush by both new and old firms to establish an online presence.

The Dot-Com Bubble Explodes (Section 2.2)

The excitement of the dot-com boom didn't last forever. Many e-commerce sites and other Internet businesses went under when the bubble broke in the early 2000s. When the market saw that online retailers' profits were not a sure thing, it experienced a severe correction.

Survival in Hard Times 2.3

Some internet stores were able to persevere and even thrive after the dot-com bubble broke. Amazon and eBay, for example, kept expanding thanks to their emphasis on the long term and the diversification of their product lines. The online retail sector's fortitude and creativity were honed throughout this difficult time.

Technological Developments and Expanding E-Commerce

3.1 Faster Connections and Broadband Internet

The rapid spread of high-speed Internet access in the early 2000s was a major factor in the development of the internet retail industry. Consumers found it less of a hassle to shop online when internet speeds and reliability improved. With the advent of high-speed internet, it became possible to broadcast images and videos of products, improving the online buying experience.

3.2 Safe Payment Processors

Safer online transactions are now possible thanks to advancements in encryption and secure payment gateways. As a result of these developments, shoppers felt more comfortable sharing their financial details on online marketplaces.

3.3.3 "M-Commerce" or "Mobile Commerce"

The proliferation of smartphones and other mobile devices has given rise to new opportunities for e-commerce. Consumers were able to shop anywhere, anytime, thanks to the rise of mobile apps and mobile-optimized websites. The proliferation of online shopping can be attributed, in part, to the advent of mobile shopping.

3.4 Online Marketplaces and Storefronts

Shopify, WooCommerce, and Magento are just a few of the e-commerce systems that have made it simpler for companies of all kinds to launch and operate their own websites. Online marketplaces like Etsy and Alibaba expanded sellers' access to buyers around the world.

Chapter 4: Consumers' Changing Habits

4.1.1 The Ease of It

The ease of online purchasing has contributed significantly to its meteoric rise. Customers' perspectives on retailing have shifted due to the advent of 24/7 online shopping accessible from the convenience of a shopper's own home or mobile device. The vast selection of goods, from commonplace necessities to specialised goods, available online contributes to this ease.

4.2 Reviews and Price Analysis

The convenience of price comparison and customer feedback is a major draw for many people to shop online. Because of this openness, shoppers are better able to compare prices and select the most advantageous option. Having review and rating options available also helps build confidence in online markets.

Customization and Suggestions 4.3

Data analytics and AI are used by online marketplaces to customise customer service. Making shopping online more interesting and increasing the possibility of conversions, product recommendations based on browsing and purchase history do just that.

4.4 Social Media and Influencers' Impact

In recent years, social media sites have become indispensable to the success of any online retailer. Brands and stores use social media to spread their message and interact with their customers. People with big online followings, or "influencers," on sites like Instagram and YouTube are crucial in advertising items and influencing consumer preferences.

The Amazon Effect (Chapter 5)

5.1 The Dominance of Amazon

Amazon, started by Jeff Bezos in 1995, is largely responsible for the rise of e-commerce. The original online bookstore gradually grew into a more diverse and extensive marketplace. Amazon is one of the major e-commerce platforms because it prioritises its customers, has well-oiled logistics, and is always innovating.

5.2 The Effect on Brick-and-Mortar Stores

The rise of online retailers like Amazon has disrupted the industry at large. Customers have switched from traditional retailers to the company's online marketplace because of the low prices, wide variety of products, and quick turnaround times on orders. It has been difficult for many brick-and-mortar stores to compete with Amazon.

Providers of Market and Order Fulfilment Services

Unlike traditional retail stores, Amazon's marketplace approach welcomes independent retailers to advertise and ship their wares to customers. By taking care of things like storage, packing, and shipping, Amazon's Fulfilment by Amazon (FBA) service has helped small and medium-sized enterprises attract customers all over the world.

Chapter 6: The Explosion of Shopping Apps for Mobile Devices
A New Era of Shopping Is Here: 6.1

Online retail has been revolutionised by mobile shopping apps. Retailers and marketplaces have poured resources into creating intuitive apps that streamline the purchasing process for customers. Consumers may shop anytime, anyplace with the push of a mobile app.

6.2 App Improvements and Features

Barcode scanning for cost comparisons, augmented reality for virtual try-ons, and one-click payment are just a few of the capabilities available in mobile shopping apps. Repeat business and participation might be prompted through push notifications and customised offers.

Mobile Payment Solutions, Section 6.3

The mobile checkout process has been simplified with the introduction of mobile payment systems like as Apple Pay, Google Pay, and digital wallets. Mobile purchasing has been further encouraged by the prevalence of these safe and handy payment methods.

The Globalisation of Electronic Commerce

7.1.1 International online trade
The advent of e-commerce has removed physical barriers, allowing companies to sell to consumers all over the globe. Possibilities made possible by international online trade

 allows sole proprietors, small enterprises, and startups to reach a worldwide market. Shopify and Etsy have made it possible for anyone to open their own online shop and sell to customers all around the world.

Global Markets and Business Competition

Increased competitiveness among companies is another effect of cross-border e-commerce. To succeed in today's global economy, businesses must respond to shifting customer demands, comply with ever-changing trade restrictions, and continually improve their offerings. As a result, several sectors have been able to innovate and specialise.

Influencer marketing and social media platforms, chapter 8.

The Influence of Social Media on Online Shopping 8.1

To conduct business online, social media sites are now necessities. Many companies today use social media to communicate with their consumers, promote new goods, and reach certain demographics. Social media sites like Facebook, Instagram, and Pinterest have made it easier for users to make purchases by incorporating tools like "Shop Now" buttons and shoppable posts.

8.2 The Impact of Influencer Marketing

For online retailers, influencer marketing has become an increasingly effective strategy. Sales are typically significantly impacted when social media influencers with huge audiences endorse products and services to their followers. The way in which brands interact with their target audiences and pique their attention has been revolutionised by this type of advertising.

User-created content (also known as UGC) 8.3

Customer evaluations and other forms of user-generated material have become increasingly valuable to online retailers. Consumers place a high value on the insights and feedback of their peers when out shopping. Online stores promote and display UGC as a means of increasing customer confidence in their brand.

Chapter 9: The Development of Financial Transactions

9.1 New Developments in Recurring Payments

Along with the rise of e-commerce, new payment mechanisms have emerged. Contactless payments, biometric authentication, and voice-activated transactions are just some of the ongoing advancements while traditional card payments remain popular. These innovations are made to strengthen safety and simplify the purchasing procedure.

9.2 Emerging Markets and Financial Inclusion

By making global online marketplaces more accessible to those living in developing countries, e-commerce has helped expand people's access to financial services. People in areas without easy access to conventional banking systems can now engage in e-commerce thanks to the proliferation of mobile banking and payment services.

Chapter 10: "Online Business and the COVID-19 Outbreak"

The Pandemic and the Explosion of Online Shopping

The 2019 COVID-19 epidemic hit late and hit e-commerce hard. Many conventional stores had to temporarily seal their doors as a result of lockdowns and other forms of social separation. In light of this, many people have started doing their shopping online instead.

10.2 Continued Expansion and Shifting Consumer Habits

E-commerce has continued to expand even as regulations have loosened because many consumers prefer the convenience of shopping from home. Consumers have shifted their shopping patterns to include more diverse online purchases, such as food and home office supplies. The retail industry's transition to digital was hastened by this change.

10.3 Opportunities and Threats

Businesses faced difficulties as a result of the pandemic, but they also had possibilities. E-commerce businesses changed to match the rising demand, and conventional stores sped up their digital initiatives. As a result of the pandemic, new innovations in contactless delivery, curbside pickup, and digital shopping experiences arose.

Future of Online Shopping (Chapter 11)

11.1 Ongoing Improvements in Technology

Online purchasing is developing rapidly. The future of this industry is being shaped by a number of trends and developments, including:

There will be an increase in the use of AI-powered personalised shopping experiences, chatbots for customer service, and cutting-edge recommendation systems.

- Augmented Reality (AR) and Virtual Reality (VR): Consumers will be able to virtually try on apparel, see products in their own homes, and have a better online shopping experience as a result of these technologies.

More and more shoppers are thinking twice about how their choices may affect the planet. In response, the e-commerce industry is implementing eco-friendly policies including carbon-neutral shipping and environmentally-friendly packaging.

- Omnichannel Retail: As companies invest in omnichannel strategy, the line between online and offline retail will continue to blur, enabling customers to easily transition between digital and physical shopping.

Globalisation will continue, and e-commerce that spans national boundaries will become easier for small and medium-sized enterprises to implement, boosting international trade.

11.2 Online Trade in Developing Economies

Expanding internet availability and rising consumer incomes give opportunities for firms in emerging economies, which will contribute to the expansion of e-commerce into these regions. Success in these areas will depend heavily on mobile-first initiatives and localised approaches.

11.3, Ethical and Regulatory Considerations

The likes of data privacy, cybersecurity, and competition will be scrutinised more closely in the future of e-commerce. Antitrust issues and consumer protection are two areas that governments and regulatory agencies will work to improve in the future of the industry.

Conclusion

The history of online buying is a fascinating exploration of how technology, business, and consumer habits have all come together. From its infancy to its current status as a worldwide sector, e-commerce has revolutionised the ways in which consumers search for, make, and receive purchases. Although the landscape of online commerce is always evolving, one thing is certain: this revolutionary force will significantly impact the ways in which people shop, do business, and communicate for the foreseeable future. The history of online buying is not a static tale; rather, it is a dynamic one that will continue to drive commerce into the future.

Chapter 2:
Creating a Virtual Storefront

2.1- Choosing a niche for your e-commerce business.

Introduction

The launch of a new online store may be a thrilling and financially rewarding experience. Because of the internet's global reach, you can do business with people all over the world who are interested in what you have to sell. However, the early decision you make—which niche to pursue—can make or break your online store.

Choosing a certain market segment to focus on is crucial because it determines your company's direction, customer base, product lineup, and promotional tactics. Here, we'll discuss in detail how to identify a market segment for your online store. We will give you with a road map to make educated decisions that will put your e-commerce enterprise on the right track, from comprehending the significance of niche selection to performing market research, recognising trends, and assessing your passion and experience.

Niche selection is stressed in the first chapter.

1.1.1 Niche Definition
When discussing online business, the term "niche" is used to describe a targeted subset of the overall market. It's a niche market where you may focus your efforts on satisfying the specific requirements of a subset of customers. Finding a market that is not too competitive but still has enough demand to keep your firm afloat is the goal of niche selection.

1.2 The Importance of Choosing a Niche

Your e-commerce firm will be profoundly affected by the niche you choose.

To differentiate yourself from the competitors in a crowded market, find a niche in which to operate.

To reach a specific demographic, you can develop advertising campaigns and wares that speak directly to them.

When there is less rivalry in a given market segment, it can be less difficult to build your brand and grow your share of the market.

- Passion and Expertise: Establishing a company in a field in which you have a deep interest or extensive understanding can be both personally rewarding and strategically advantageous.

(1) The Dangers of Not Specialising
Problems can arise, such as those listed below, if you don't narrow your focus and instead aim for the masses.
- Intense Competition: It might be challenging to stand out and establish a presence in oversaturated marketplaces.

- Expensive Marketing Expenses: Targeting a large audience can be time-consuming and expensive.

Lack of Focus: If your company doesn't have a specific target audience, it may be hard to create a memorable brand name and logo.

Chapter 2: Recognising Your Interests and Capabilities

The Importance of Passion (2.1)

Picking a speciality is greatly influenced by personal interest. Your interest in and enthusiasm for a certain field or subject matter can serve as a powerful source of inspiration for your online store's success. Products, interactions with customers, and marketing initiatives will all benefit from your excitement.

Using Knowledgeable Resources 2.2

Having specialised knowledge or expertise can help your online store succeed. You may use your knowledge to find great suppliers, write engaging content, and earn the loyalty of consumers who value your insights.

Aligning Interests and Capabilities for Financial Success

Expertise and fervour are great, but only if they help bring in money. Unfortunately, not everyone can turn their interests or talents into a successful online store. Checking the market potential and demand in your chosen sector is essential.

Market Analysis and Research (3)

Market Opportunities 3.1

Finding niches or unfulfilled requirements in a market is a key part of conducting successful market research. Find places where there is a dearth of innovation or where customers are unhappy with the current offerings.

3.2 Research on the Competition

Competitor analysis can help you learn about the opportunities and threats facing organisations in your industry. It also aids in pinpointing areas for specialisation and development.

3.3.3 Search Engine Optimisation

Finding out what people in your target market are typing into search engines to find solutions to their problems requires extensive keyword research. E-commerce sites that employ efficient SEO (search engine optimisation) tactics tend to perform better in SERPs.

3.4 Trends and Consumer Behaviour

It is essential to keep up with customer trends and behaviour in your specialty. Your product decisions, price points, and advertising strategies can all benefit from these observations.

Chapter 4: Assessing Consumer Interest

The Size and Development of the Market (Section 4.1)

It's crucial to know how big your target market is and how fast it's expected to expand. It can be difficult to sustain rapid expansion in an online store if your target market is very narrow and unchanging.

4.2 Analysis of the Intended Readership

Determine who you want to reach out to in your specific expertise. Create a thorough buyer persona by thinking about their demographics, psychographics, and purchasing habits. You can use this persona to direct your marketing and product development activities.

The Market Demand Test (Section 4.3)
Do some market research before you commit to a specific specialty. You can gauge interest in a product by accepting pre-orders or conducting a crowdfunding campaign on a modest scale.

Chapter 5: "Picking Profitable Market Niche"

Trend Analysis 5.1

The term "trending niche" refers to a market segment that is seeing increased activity and demand. While keeping an eye out for trends can be helpful, it's important to consider whether or not those patterns will last.

5.2 Trend Analysis Resources

You can find hot markets and items with the help of a variety of web resources. In order to analyse trends, tools like Google Trends, social media listening platforms, and online marketplaces are quite helpful.

5.3.1 Finding a Sweet Spot Between Hot and Evergreen Niche Markets

While hot markets provide potential for rapid expansion, it's wise to diversify your business into "evergreen" markets as well. Stability and expansion possibilities can be provided by a combination of trending and evergreen niches.

Monetization Techniques and Business Plans

Monetization strategies 6.1

Think about how you'll make money off of your specialised online store. Sales of goods and services, subscription models, affiliate marketing, and advertising are all common ways to generate income.

Pricing Strategies, Section 6.2

The niche and demographic you're aiming for should inform your price strategy. Make a decision as to how you will compete in the market: price, quality, or value.

Analysing Profit Margins, Section 6.3

Think about the margins of profit you could make in your target market. Profitability can be estimated by adding up the predicted income, operating expenses, and cost of goods sold (COGS).
Differentiation and Branding, Section 7

Formulating a Differentiating Selling Proposition (DSP) 7.1
Your e-commerce firm's USP is what makes it stand out from the crowd. It ought to connect with your ideal clientele and convey the exceptional value you provide.
Branding and Storytelling, Section 7.2

Creating a memorable brand identity and story may strengthen your relationship with clients. Your brand should convey your genuine interest in and understanding of your speciality.

Establishing Reliability and Trustworthiness

In the digital marketplace, trust is king. Building trust and reputation in your area can be accomplished by measures such as providing access to honest user feedback, offering safe payment methods, and providing first-rate customer service.

Part 8: Supply Chain Management and Procurement

8.1 Product or Service Sourcing

Depending on your specialty, you may need to acquire materials, software, or labour. Think about using wholesalers, manufacturers, dropshippers, or even making your own products.

8.2 Inventory Control

Overstocking or running out of products can be avoided with careful inventory management. You may improve the efficiency of your supply chain by using reorder points and inventory tracking systems.

Shipping and Fulfilment 8.3

Think about the logistics of order processing and shipping. In-house fulfilment, 3PL suppliers, and e-commerce platforms that offer fulfilment services are all viable options.

Chapter 9: Putting Together an Online Store.

Selecting an Online Storefront (Section 9.1)

Pick an online store solution that works for your specific market and company goals. Shopify, BigCommerce, and WordPress' WooCommerce are just a few of your choices. Think on how flexible, adaptable, and scalable the solution is.

9.2 User Experience (UX) and Website Design

Create an e-commerce website that is both easy to navigate and aesthetically pleasing. Be consistent with your brand's aesthetic and make it easy for customers to make purchases.

Mobile Optimisation (9.3)

Mobile optimisation should be a top priority in light of the rise of mobile commerce. Your e-commerce platform needs to be mobile-friendly and responsive.

Part TEN: Advertising and Publicity

Creating a Promotional Strategy 10.1

Make sure you're reaching out to the right people by developing a detailed marketing strategy. Think about search engine optimisation (SEO), paid advertising, email marketing, social media marketing, and content marketing.

10.2 Blogging and Content Production

Using content marketing, you may build credibility as an authority in your field. Produce high-quality material including blog articles, videos, and guides on a consistent basis.

Engaging with Social Media 10.3

Use online communities to talk to your target market. To expand your audience, it's important to provide useful material, engage with your followers, and make use of social media advertising.

Expanding and Saturating Your Online Store, Chapter 11

11.1 Sizing Up Development Prospects

Consider expansion options when your online store gets established. Increasing product variety, penetrating untapped markets, and introducing new revenue streams are all viable options.

11.2 Iteration and Customer Feedback

E-commerce businesses may learn a lot by collecting and analysing client feedback. Improve your offerings and your customers' overall experience by listening to their suggestions.

11.3 Responsible Scaling

Managing your resources effectively and strategically is essential for expanding your online store's operations. Make sure you can keep up with demand without sacrificing product quality, customer service, or operational efficiency.

Chapter 12: Obstacles and Potential Traps

Risk Factors 12.1

Selecting a profitable e-commerce specialty is not without its difficulties. Don't make the frequent mistakes of picking a market niche based only on what's popular, skipping over market research, and underestimating the competitors.

Adaptability and adaptability 12.2

Due to the ever-changing nature of the e-commerce industry, unexpected obstacles may occur. The market and buyer habits are constantly shifting, so remain flexible.

Conclusion

Identifying a certain market to focus on when starting an online store is crucial. Passion, knowledge, market analysis, and business sense are all necessary ingredients. If you follow the advice in this article, you'll be able to make smart decisions that will help your online store thrive. Keep in mind that choosing a niche is not a static process, but rather one that should develop as your knowledge of the e-commerce industry grows. Your e-commerce enterprise has the ability to succeed in the highly competitive online market with hard work, careful planning, and a focus on providing value to your target demographic.

2.2- Selecting the right e-commerce platform.

Introduction

Choosing the best e-commerce platform in today's rapidly changing retail environment is crucial to the long-term health and growth of your online store. It can be challenging to choose the best platform among the many accessible because they all serve distinct purposes. Learn how to choose the best e-commerce platform for your specific business with the help of this detailed guide. We will help you make a well-informed decision by examining key features, scalability, security, and cost in light of your unique business needs and goals.

The Importance of Selecting the Appropriate E-Commerce Platform

1.1 The Backbone of Your eCommerce Shop

Your online store can't get off the ground without first deciding on an e-commerce platform. It has consequences for your website's performance, your customers' experience, your ability to accept payments, and your daily operations. The opposite is true as well: a platform that isn't a good fit can cause inefficiencies and prevent growth.

Ability to Grow and Last for the Future 1.2
The best e-commerce platform will be flexible enough to expand as your company does. Scalability guarantees that your platform can handle an increase in users, products, and transactions without requiring a complete redesign.

Advantage in the Market, Version 1.3

Having an advantage over the competition is possible with the correct platform choice. Provide a streamlined purchasing experience, cater to mobile consumers, and boost customer engagement and loyalty with the help of this.

The second chapter is titled "Assessing Your Business Needs and Objectives."

Business Model Understanding 2.1

Identifying your business model is the first step in selecting the best e-commerce platform. Do you want to sell only digital products, only physical things, or a mix of both? Do you want or need elements like memberships, auctions, or recurring payments?

Market and Audience Specifics 2.2

Platform choice is heavily influenced by your target market and audience. Think about where your customers are located, what they like, and how they shop when making decisions. Some markets and demographics may be better served by one platform over another.
2.3 Organisational Aims and Priorities

Establish both near-term and long-term targets for your company. Is your goal sustained expansion into new markets or the establishment of a dominant position in a subset of the market? The ideal platform will help you achieve your objectives and realise your company's vision.

Part Three: E-Commerce Platform Categories

Platforms: Hosted vs. Self-Hosted (3.1)

Understand the key differences between hosted and self-hosted e-commerce solutions. Shopify and BigCommerce are two examples of hosted platforms that offer ease but may limit personalization. Self-hosted platforms, like as WooCommerce, give you more freedom but necessitate technical knowledge.

Open-source versus Closed-Source Systems 3.2

Recognise the distinction between open-source and proprietary systems. Open-source platforms like Magento and WooCommerce are flexible and provide you more power, but they can be more difficult to set up and maintain. Shopify and Squarespace are two proprietary platforms that are easy to use but lack the flexibility of WordPress.

3.3 Targeted Host Machines

There are specialised e-commerce sites that serve particular markets. Some marketplaces, like Etsy, specialise on vintage and handmade items, while others, like Gumroad, sell only digital products. Think about whether or not your company would benefit from using niche platforms.

Key Features and Functionality (Chapter 4)

4.1 Essential Components of an Online Store

Think about things like product catalogue management, inventory tracking, shopping cart features, and safe payment processing when you evaluate potential e-commerce platforms. Your online shop wouldn't be much without these essential elements.

4.2.1 Adaptability to Mobile Devices

An increasing number of transactions are being made via mobile devices. Make sure the platform you go with is responsive to mobile devices, so that people can have a great experience with it on their phones and tablets. Think about options that are unique to mobile devices, such as mobile wallets and one-click purchases.

Optimisation for Search Engines (SEO) Capabilities 4.3

If you want people to find your online store organically, SEO is a must. Best practises for search engine optimisation (SEO), such as user-friendly URLs, meta tags, and a sitemap, should be supported by your platform.

4.4 Performance and Scalability

To accommodate expansion, scalability is essential. Analyse the platform to see if it can handle an increasing product catalogue without slowing down or otherwise impacting the user experience.

Security and Regulations (Chapter 5)

Payment Guarantees, Section 5.1

Safety is of utmost importance when conducting business online. Verify that PCI DSS compliance has been implemented throughout the platform. In addition, make sure there are safeguards like SSL certificates, encryption, and safe payment options.

5.2 Privacy and Data Security

Protect personal information in accordance with state and federal laws including the California Consumer Privacy Act and the General Data Protection Regulation. Determine if the platform has data protection and client consent management solutions that make it easier to comply with regulations.

5.3.1 Ongoing Maintenance and Fixes

Over time, security flaws may become more prevalent. Pick a system that swiftly addresses security flaws with updates and patches. Keeping your consumers and company safe requires timely updates.

Chapter 6: Putting It All Together and Making It Your Own

6.1 Integrations with Other Services

Check the platform's ability to integrate with your preferred payment processor, shipping company, and marketing automation software. Your platform's potential is limited only by the number and quality of its integrations.

6.2 Configurable Features

Think about the flexibility of the platform. Can the look and feel as well as the features be altered to fit your brand and business requirements? Determine if the system allows for the addition of custom code.

6.3 Support for APIs and Programmers
Evaluate the API (Application Programming Interface) capabilities and the availability of developer assistance and resources if you need in-depth customization or integration with proprietary systems.
User Experience and Design (Chapter 7)

Templates & Website Design, Version 7.1

The aesthetic quality of your online store is important. The platform's design themes and templates should be examined to verify they may be modified to fit your needs and those of your business.

7.2 An Easy-to-Navigate Layout

Conversion rates are heavily dependent on the user experience (UX). To effectively run your store, use a system that has an easy-to-navigate backend interface.

Receptive Layout 7.4

Your website will have a consistent appearance and feel across all devices and screen sizes thanks to responsive design. See how well the platform works on various screen sizes, especially those of mobile devices and tablets.

Support and Community, Chapter 8.

8.1 Support for Customers

It's crucial to have dependable and fast client service. Live chat, email, and phone assistance are just some of the customer service channels that should be evaluated. Think about the hours of operation of your firm in comparison to the platform's support availability.

8.2 Social Networks and Available Tools

It can be helpful to have a lively user community and entry to learning materials. In order to get the most out of a platform, it should have user support in the form of forums, knowledge bases, webinars, and tutorials.

8.3 Sla (Service Level Agreement)

Review the service level agreements (SLAs) provided by the platform to understand the promises about availability, response times, and issue resolution if your business depends largely on the platform's uptime and support.

Chapter 9: Financial Factors

Initial Investment 9.1

Think about how much money you'll need to get started with things like a platform, a domain name, and a customised design. While some platforms may need a sizable upfront expenditure, others may offer free trials or reduced charges.

9.2 Ongoing Fees and Maintenance

Think about the monthly subscription fees, transaction fees, and hosting costs associated with your platform of choice. Your long-term profitability may be impacted by these costs.

9.3 Costs of Scalability

The platform's fees could rise as your company expands. Think about the long-term viability of your pricing strategy by analysing how it scales with the expansion of your business.

Chapter 10: Deciding Wisely

Analysis, Comparative

Compare and contrast several online storefronts to choose the best one for your business. Start by making a list of everything you need to run your business. Analyse how well each service fits these criteria.

10.2 Reviews and Feedback from Users

It's a good idea to research the platforms you're thinking of using by reading customer evaluations and getting input from other online retailers. Perspectives gained from actual life events are often more insightful.

10.3 Testing and Experimental Phases

Make the most of free trials and introductory periods provided by online storefronts wherever possible. You can determine if the platform is a good fit for your company's needs by trying it out for yourself.

Migration and Deployment, Section Eleven

Migrating Data 11.1

Data migration must be planned for in advance of any migration from an existing platform. Find out if the platform you're considering has any migration tools or services.

Strategy for Implementation 11.2

Create a migration plan that specifies who will do what and when during the transition to the new platform. Your business operations should be interrupted as little as possible thanks to this approach.
Testing and Quality Control (11.3)
Before going live, make sure the new e-commerce platform has been thoroughly tested. Find and fix problems with the product's usability, aesthetics, and/or functionality.

Evaluation and Improvement Following Implementation (Chapter 12)

12.1 Tracking How Well You're Doing

Maintain constant vigilance after opening your online store. Use analytics software to monitor KPIs like conversion rates, page views, and revenue.

Getting Input From Users and Iterating

Listen to your clients and other interested parties to learn where you might make changes. You can use this information to make adjustments to your website's layout, features, and overall user experience.

Optimising on a Continuous Basis 12.3

Improve the effectiveness of your online store with constant A/B testing, search engine optimisation (SEO), and conversion rate optimisation (CRO).

Protecting Your eCommerce Enterprise From the Future

13.1 Flexibility in the Face of New Technologies

The tools used in online stores are always getting better. Make sure the platform you choose is flexible enough to accommodate future developments in areas like mobile commerce, voice commerce, and augmented reality.

Planning for Scalability and Expansion 13.2

Consider the long run by picking a system that can expand with your company. Things like exploring new markets, increasing production capacity, and introducing new products are all part of this.

13.3 Adaptability to Emerging Demands

Demands in the business world are always evolving. Pick a system that will let you make changes to your e-commerce approach, implement new features, and shift gears as needed.

Chapter 14: The Wrap-Up

Your company's growth, expansion, and competitiveness are all dependent on your choice of e-commerce platform. Make a well-informed decision that helps you achieve your business goals and objectives by first gaining a complete grasp of your needs, then comparing and contrasting key features, and finally thinking about security and compliance while keeping costs in mind.

Keep in mind that your e-commerce platform is an adaptable and changeable part of your organisation that may change as the market and technology do. If you want your e-commerce firm to survive and thrive into the future, you need to regularly evaluate its performance, get customer input, and keep up with developing trends.

You can use the power of the proper e-commerce platform to drive the success and growth of your online business by providing your customers with a pleasurable and stress-free purchasing experience.

2.3- Designing and launching a user-friendly website.

Introduction

In today's technological world, having a website that is easy to navigate is crucial. Whether you're running an online store and want more customers, a blog and want more readers, or a charity and want to make more connections with donors, a well-designed and user-friendly website is your virtual storefront and first impression.

This all-inclusive manual will lead you through the maze of website creation and rollout with ease. The knowledge and practical steps to create a website that not only looks great but also offers an exceptional user experience will be provided, from understanding the principles of web design to defining your website's purpose and audience to planning your site structure and content to optimising for mobile and ensuring security.

The Value of an Easy-to-Navigate Website (Chapter 1)

Digital Iconic First Impression 1.1

Customers, readers, and donors may encounter your company for the first time on your website. A good first impression can be made by a user-friendly website, while a negative one can be formed by one that is difficult to navigate.
1.2.1 Improving the User Interface (UI)
Maintaining traffic and accomplishing your site's objectives depend on providing a positive user experience (UX). A user-friendly website makes it simple for visitors to get about, participate, and locate what they're looking for.

1.3 Visibility in Search Engines

Websites that are easy to navigate are given higher ranks by search engines like Google. Better search engine rankings and more organic visitors can be achieved by making your website more user-friendly.

Identifying Your Website's Goals and Visitors is Covered in Chapter 2

2.1 Objectives and Aims That Are Specified

You should decide what you want your website to do before you start building it. Do you want to raise money, spread knowledge, organise a group, or sell something? Design decisions are made with the purpose in mind.

2.2 Target Market Research

Knowing who you're writing for is essential. Develop in-depth customer personas to learn more about your target audience's motivations, goals, and pain areas. Make sure your website is adjusted to cover these points.

2.3 Market Research

Look at the websites of your niche's rivals and figure out what makes them tick. Take note of their accomplishments and watch out for their mistakes.

Web Design Basics (Chapter 3)

Receptive Layout 3.0

With responsive design, your website will look great and perform smoothly on any device, from mobile phones to desktop computers. With the rise in mobile traffic, it is essential to optimise for mobile devices.

3.2 User-Friendly Layout and Menus

Users should be able to quickly find the content or goods they need by navigating a simple menu. Keep things simple and don't overlink.

3.3 Design Element Consistency

Consistency in colour scheme, typeface, and other visual aspects conveys competence and reliability. To ensure consistency, use a style guide.

Chapter 4: Laying the Foundation for Your Website

Sitemap Development 4.1.1

Your website's structure can be seen in a sitemap. Make a site map to make sure your site is easy to use.

User Flow and Navigation 4.2

Think about the typical user flow through your site. Make sure they can easily navigate between pages and complete the appropriate actions.

Wireframing and prototyping, section 4.3

You can see the site's structure and functions more clearly with the help of a wireframe or prototype. In terms of usability testing and improvement, they are priceless.

Content Creation and Strategy (Chapter 5)

Planning Content 5.1

The text, photographs, videos, and other media that will make up your website's content must be identified. Make a content calendar to plan ahead.

5.2 Generation of Valuable Content

Having content of a high standard is mandatory. Create content that is engaging, informative, and error-free. Spend money on expert photos and layout.

The importance of accessibility and inclusion, 5.3

Make sure your content can be accessed by everyone, including individuals with special needs. Use the guidelines established by the Web Content Accessibility Guidelines (WCAG).

The Creation of a Website (Chapter 6)

Selecting a Host System 6.1

Choose a web host that works well for your goals and level of expertise. WordPress, Wix, Squarespace, and custom-built sites are just a few of the most popular alternatives.

Hosting 6.2 Websites

Pick a hosting service that you can trust for speed, safety, and expansion. Think about things like data storage, transfer rates, and availability.

Choosing a Template (Version 6.3)

You can save time and energy by starting with a premade website template. Make it fit your individual style.

Designing the User Interface (UI)

7.1 Aspects of Visual Design

Focus on the visuals, including the colour palette, font, and picture selection. Make a consistent and aesthetically pleasing user interface.

7.2 Positioning of Calls to Action (CTAs)

Put calls to action in strategic locations to encourage users to take the actions you want them to take, such as purchasing, subscribing, or getting in touch.

Intuitive Forms 7.3

Create user-friendly forms that won't put people off. Don't waffle; give precise, succinct directions.

Optimisation for Mobile Devices
8.2 Mobile-First Methodology

Keep mobile users in mind when designing. Make sure your website works properly across all devices by testing it on as many as possible.

8.2 Navigation Optimised for Mobile Devices

Make it easier for mobile users to navigate. Think about creating mobile-friendly menus and expandable content.

8.3 Performance and Page Speed

Compressing pictures, minifying code, and decreasing server calls will all help your site operate better on mobile devices.

Testing and Quality Control (Chapter 9)

9.1 Compatibility with Various Browsers

Make that your site works and looks the same on several browsers (Chrome, Firefox, Safari, Edge, etc.).

9.2 User Evaluation

Conduct usability tests with actual end users to get their comments. Determine where they are having difficulty and address those issues.

Performance Evaluations 9.3

Use third-party resources like Google PageSpeed Insights and GTmetrix to gauge how well your website performs. Fix the things that are slowing down the loading and loading times.

SEO and Online Visibility (10th Chapter)

10.2 On-Page SEO

Optimise the page's title, meta description, headers, and alt text to improve its search engine rankings. Integrate proper keyword usage into the flow of your writing.

10.2 SEO Site Architecture

Make a search engine optimised (SEO) URL structure that includes relevant keywords in each URL. Make sure your site has good navigation and SEO by using internal links.

10.3 Regional SEO

Local search engine optimisation is essential if you have a physical location. Make a Google My Business page, make sure it's verified, and start soliciting feedback from nearby customers.

Security and Personal Information Protection

11.1 Secure Sockets Layer

Installing an SSL (Secure Sockets Layer) certificate on your website will encrypt user data in transit and inspire confidence in your site's safety.

Assure Regular Backups (11.2)

Prepare for the possibility of data loss due to technical faults or cyberattacks by setting up automated backups of your website's data.

Security Add-ons and Real-Time Reporting 11.3

Protect your website from potential dangers by using security plugins or technologies. Maintain constant vigilance for any untoward behaviour.

The Website Launching Process (Chapter 12)
Final Examination 12.1.

Test everything one last time to make sure it's operating properly. Make sure there are no broken buttons, forms, or other features.

12.1 Pre-Deployment Checklist

Make sure you have completed all of the necessary steps before launching your website, such as implementing analytics, submitting your sitemap to search engines, and setting up 301 redirects.

Moving Content 12.3

Make sure everything goes well and that all links point where they need to go if you're moving material from an older site.

new domain.

Optimisation and Upkeep Following Launch (Chapter 13)

Monitoring and Analytics 13.1

Use analytics tools to keep an eye on how well your website is doing. Keep an eye on things like visitors, sales, and pageviews.

13.2 New and Updated Content

Keep your information current and interesting by updating it frequently. Get rid of all the old stuff and the links that don't work.

Updates to Security Measures 13.3

Always be wary about your safety. Always use the most recent versions of your platform, themes, and plugins.

Chapter 14: "Input from Users and Iterative Development"

14.1 Gathering Input From Customers

Get them to fill out surveys, contact forms, or use social media to share their thoughts. Pay attention to what they have to say and how they feel.

Improvements Made Iteratively 14.2

Make incremental updates to your site based on user feedback. Take into account user feedback and make adjustments to improve usability.

Chapter 15: The Wrap-Up

Developing and releasing a user-friendly website is an iterative procedure that calls for forethought, originality, and persistence. It is important that your website accurately represents your company, that it is easy to navigate, and that it helps you reach your business objectives.

If you follow the guidelines and suggestions in this manual, you should be able to build a website that not only attracts users but also keeps them interested and satisfied. Always keep in mind that your audience's demands and expectations are subject to change as the digital world develops, and make adjustments to your website accordingly.

You may connect with your target audience, gain their trust, and eventually find success in the digital world with the help of a user-friendly website.

Chapter 3:
Strategies for Online Stores

3.1- Exploring various e-commerce business models (B2C, B2B, dropshipping, etc.).

Businesses and consumers alike have benefited greatly from the advent of e-commerce. As the online market grows, entrepreneurs are adopting new business models to meet the needs of a wide variety of customers. In order to make educated selections and settle on a strategy that is a good fit for your goals and resources, you need to be familiar with the various e-commerce business models.

Direct sales from companies to consumers, also known as business-to-consumer (B2C) e-commerce.

The most prevalent type of online commercial transaction is business-to-consumer (B2C) e-commerce. The key elements of this method are an easy-to-navigate internet business, smart advertising, and smooth financial dealings. The success of business-to-consumer (B2C) enterprises depends on attracting and retaining consumers, hence B2C organisations place a premium on customer service. Amazon, Shopify, and other B2C e-commerce success stories include online fashion companies.

Second, B2B e-commerce focuses on serving the needs of other businesses rather than consumers.

In business-to-business (B2B) e-commerce, one organisation sells goods or services to another for the latter's internal use or for resale. Business-to-business (B2B) networks simplify collaboration, negotiations, and large-scale transactions. Larger-scale transactions are usual for this paradigm, which is used frequently by wholesale and manufacturing companies. Business-to-business (B2B) e-commerce facilitates effective sourcing, inventory management, and supplier collaboration. Examples of successful B2B e-commerce platforms include Alibaba and ThomasNet.

Third, dropshipping is a low-capital, low-risk business model.

In the dropshipping model of online retailing, the retailer has no physical inventory of goods for sale. When a product is sold, the merchant often will not stock it, but will instead order it from a supplier and have it transported directly to the consumer. The model reduces the overhead and complexity of managing inventory. Marketing, customer service, and establishing reliable relationships with reliable suppliers are the main focuses of a dropshipping company. Although there are less obstacles to entrance, you'll need dependable suppliers and a solid marketing plan to be successful in dropshipping. Common choices for dropshipping firms include Shopify and Oberlo.

Fourth, recurring income from e-commerce subscriptions.

In subscription-based e-commerce arrangements, customers sign up to receive recurring shipments of a product or service at regular intervals. This method increases customer loyalty and guarantees steady income. This approach has been implemented by companies in many other industries, from meal kits to streaming services. Successful subscription businesses, such as Netflix and Blue Apron, cater to their customers' individual tastes to guarantee recurring revenue and customer satisfaction.

P2P e-commerce 5: Empowering Individuals

Peer-to-peer (P2P) e-commerce platforms eliminate the need for middlemen by connecting buyers and sellers online. These sites serve as virtual malls where vendors may post their wares, consumers can browse them, and deals can be made. The community-based structure of P2P e-commerce is what makes it unique, allowing users to make money off of their unused skills, goods, or talents. Etsy is an online marketplace for handmade goods, while Airbnb is a similar platform for short-term lodging. In order to promote smooth transactions, P2P systems place a premium on customer trust and satisfaction.

Omnichannel e-commerce: a natural progression between online and offline markets

With omnichannel e-commerce, customers are able to shop conveniently across many channels—in-store, online, and via mobile apps and social media. This method unites the best of online and offline shopping experiences by facilitating consumers' research, purchases, and support across channels. Omnichannel techniques have been adopted by retail giants like Walmart and Target to improve consumer engagement and drive more sales. A strong inventory management system, real-time data synchronisation, and brand consistency are all essential to the success of omnichannel e-commerce.

7. Social Commerce: Marketing Products and Services on Social Networking Sites

The term "social commerce" refers to the use of online social networks for commercial purposes. By fusing the worlds of social networking and online shopping, "social commerce" lets companies market to clients, sell goods, and take payments without ever leaving the app. This strategy takes advantage of the large number of social media users and the persuasive potential of peer endorsement to help products gain widespread attention. Businesses may make money off of social media with the use of platforms like Facebook Marketplace, Instagram Shopping, and Pinterest Buyable Pins, which allow them to turn their audience into customers.

Conclusion

Companies operating in the dynamic field of e-commerce can pick from a wide variety of models, each with its own set of pros and cons. Successful business owners take the time to weigh the needs of their target market, their resources, and their expertise before deciding on a business strategy. Successful online businesses are built on a foundation of knowledge of various business models, such as business-to-consumer (B2C), business-to-business (B2B), and dropshipping.

Different e-commerce models call for different approaches to marketing, customer service, supply chain management, and tech integration. Business success in today's global, competitive digital marketplace requires an understanding of, and an openness to, a wide variety of e-commerce models. The key to growth, customer satisfaction, and long-term success rests in matching the chosen model with the company's strengths, resources, and long-term goals.

3.2- Aligning your business model with your target audience and goals.

Aligning your business model with your target audience and goals is a crucial strategic step in the ever-changing world of business. Having a clear understanding of your target market's wants, needs, and expectations, as well as the goals you hope to accomplish, can help you develop a solid business model. The necessity of this alignment is discussed, as well as methods for achieving it and case studies of companies that have successfully aligned their business models with their intended audience and objectives.

The Importance of Proper Alignment

There are a number of reasons why it's critical for your company model, audience, and objectives to all be in sync with one another:

Customer-centricity, or the practise of designing products and services with the consumer in mind, is the first step to success. Taking such a client-focused strategy boosts your chances of gaining and keeping consumers.

Second, you'll be able to manage your resources more effectively because your business strategy is consistent. When you have a firm grasp on who you're selling to and what they like, you can put your money where it will do the most good in marketing, new product development, and customer service.

3. Competitive Advantage: Knowing who you're selling to gives you an edge over the competition. Customising your business model to relieve specific problems or deliver exceptional value gives you an edge over the competition.

Your business plan should be based on your organization's aims. When your business's operations and marketing are both aligned, you increase the likelihood that you will succeed. The chances of succeeding are boosted in this way.

Methods for Harmonisation

First, you must conduct thorough research about your target demographic. Spend some time learning about the demographics, psychographics, behaviours, and pain points of your intended audience. Collect useful information through conducting surveys, interviews, analysing data from social media, and studying the market.

Developing Personas: Model specific members of your target market as Buyer Personas. Age, gender, interests, challenges, and purchase habits should all be accounted for in these fictional characters. A clear picture of your target audience can be gleaned from your personas.

Value Proposition 3: Create something that speaks to the wants and needs of your market. Explain how your offerings will help them achieve their goals and solve their difficulties.

Adjust your goods or services so that they better suit the needs of your target market. Customer input and demand will inform any necessary adjustments to features, pricing, or packaging.

5. Marketing: Create a plan for promoting your business that will appeal to its intended demographic. The key to successfully reaching your audience is picking the correct channels, messages, and content types. Focus your advertising initiatives on solving their problems and satisfying their ambitions.

Customer Feedback Loop: Create a two-way line of communication with your target market. You can learn more about client satisfaction and opportunities for growth by encouraging reviews, surveys, and open lines of contact. Take this criticism as a chance to improve your business plan.

Consistency with Organisational Objectives Make sure your business objectives fit in with those you think you're reaching. It's important to set SMART goals that can be tracked and evaluated along the way. Check in on your progress towards these targets frequently to make course corrections.

Examples of Effective Alignment

Apple Inc. (1): Apple's business plan caters to the needs of its customers by providing innovative, straightforward technologies. They place a premium on originality, aesthetics, and making the user experience as pleasant as possible. Because of this coordination, Apple has become one of the world's most valuable technology corporations.

Second, Zappos: Zappos is a company whose business model is built around providing outstanding customer service. To attract customers who value convenience when making purchases online, they provide perks like free delivery, no-hassle returns, and round-the-clock help desk staff. Zappos's success and consumer loyalty can be directly attributed to this congruence.

Third, Tesla: Tesla's business model is in line with people who care about the environment and want to support sustainable transportation. They make state-of-the-art electric vehicles with a focus on lowering carbon emissions, which should resonate with a demographic worried about global warming and open to new ideas.

Four, Airbnb: Airbnb's business approach is in sync with vacationers looking for offbeat and inexpensive lodging. They serve as a matchmaker between people who are willing to rent out their properties and visitors who are interested in unique excursions. This partnership upended the conventional hotel business and won over devoted customers.

5. Patreon: Patreon is a platform for content creators whose business model is in sync with that of artists, musicians, and creators who are looking for a reliable means of financial support. They have a subscription service that lets people financially back their favourite artists. This synergy allows artists to earn money from their creations while also giving their fans access to unique material.

Conclusion

Keeping your business strategy in sync with your intended market and end goals is an ever-evolving endeavour. You need to know your customers through and out, be willing to change things up frequently, and always put the customer first. Companies that have their models perfectly tuned to their target demographic not only win over new clients but also keep their existing ones.

Keep in mind that alignment is a process, not an event. To keep your model relevant, it is important to frequently assess customer feedback, market conditions, and company goals. Doing so will set you up for long-term success, increased customer loyalty, and the achievement of your business objectives.

Chapter 4:
Establishing a Powerful Online Identity

4.1- The importance of branding in e-commerce.

Branding is essential in today's crowded e-commerce landscape because it helps companies stand out from the crowd and form meaningful relationships with their target audiences. Branding is about more than just making a logo or phrase; it's about the overall identity, perception, and experience of a firm. The importance of branding in online business will be discussed in detail, along with the elements of a winning brand strategy and case studies of organisations that have successfully used branding strategies.

The Importance of Branding in the E-Commerce Industry

1. Differentiation: There are a lot of companies selling comparable products or services on online marketplaces. Having a memorable brand makes your company stand out from the crowd and in the minds of consumers. It helps you develop a distinguishable persona.

Second, there is an air of reliability and dependability surrounding a well-known brand. Customers are more inclined to purchase from, and continue supporting, a well-known and respected brand. Trust in your products and services can be boosted through solid branding.
Thirdly, a Emotional Connection is Created between the Brand and the Buyer. Customers are more likely to feel a strong connection to a brand if they identify with its values, stories, or mission.
4. Perceived Value: Strong branding can affect how much customers are willing to pay for your goods and services. Customers will pay more for a well-known brand because they know they will receive the expected quality, dependability, and desirability.

5. Customer Loyalty: Establishing a reliable brand fosters devoted patronage. Customers are more loyal and willing to spread the word

about your business if they have a good experience with your products or services.

Sixthly, Consistency and Recognition: A recognisable brand is one whose identity is consistent across all marketing channels. Even in a congested market, consumers will have no trouble remembering your brand.

Factors Crucial to an Effective Online Store Brand Strategy

First, Define Your Brand: Establish your brand's character as your first step. The goals, ideals, character, and tone of your company all fall under this category. How do you want people to think of your company and its products?

Make a logo that stands out and develop a visual identity using things like colour palettes and typefaces and recurring images. These components should convey your brand's values and appeal to your intended market.

3. Customer Persona: Construct in-depth representations of your ideal clientele to learn more about their needs, wants, and motivations. To appeal to your target audience, you should modify your brand's messaging and products accordingly.

Create brand message that is both clear and compelling. Taglines, mission statements, and product descriptions should all resonate with your target market and convey your brand's value proposition.

5. User Experience: Make sure your e-commerce site is easy to navigate and operates without any hiccups. Website usability includes aspects such as ease of navigation, mobile friendliness, and speed of page load.

6. material Strategy: Create a plan for publishing material that reflects the values of your company. Using your brand's voice,

produce blog entries, videos, and social media material that will educate, entertain, and inspire your target audience.

The reputation of your business can only grow if your customers have a positive experience with your company's customer service department. Get back to people quickly, help them out when they have problems, and show them some compassion.

8. Social Media: Keep a strong presence on the various social media sites used by your target demographic. Put out there material that represents your brand and gets people talking.
9. Reviews and Testimonials: Solicit and highlight reviews and testimonies from satisfied customers. Having happy customers leave reviews can do wonders for your company's reputation.
Make sure that your brand's voice is consistent in everything from your website and social media to your packaging. Consistency is the cornerstone of a recognisable brand.

Online Retail Branding Success Stories

Nike: The name Nike itself conjures images of excellence in sports and technological advancement. Throughout the world, their "Just Do It" phrase has come to represent courage and self-reliance. Nike is the undisputed leader in athletic wear, and it maintains this status by regular deployment of brand language that motivates and encourages players and sports fans.

Two, Apple: Apple stands for modern style, cutting-edge technology, and user-friendliness. The company's logo and packaging, for example, are both tasteful and straightforward. Apple has built a fan base that eagerly awaits the release of new products.

Third, Amazon: Amazon has become a household name by prioritising its customers' needs above all else. Their corporate identity, including their logo, website design, and Prime membership programme, conveys trustworthiness and a commitment to their customers. Customers know they can trust Amazon to help them discover what they need quickly and easily because of the company's branding.

Warby Parker, an online glasses store, has made a name for itself as a more accessible and ethical alternative to more established brands. They've built a dedicated consumer base because to their low prices and "Buy a Pair, Give a Pair" programme for eyeglasses.

The handmade and vintage items marketplace Etsy has built a brand around the values of craftsmanship, uniqueness, and creativity. Both consumers searching for one-of-a-kind items and merchants who place a premium on individuality will appreciate their branding.

Conclusion

Branding, in the cutthroat world of e-commerce, is much more than a logo or catchphrase; it's the whole essence of your company. What you promise your clients, how you make them feel, and what you stand for are all aspects of your brand. E-commerce brands that successfully differentiate themselves, earn customer trust and loyalty, and attract repeat customers enjoy more long-term success thanks to this strategy.

Building a brand that people love and remember takes careful consideration of your brand's identity, consistency across all brand touchpoints, and genuine interaction with your target audience. Investing correctly in your brand will pay off in the form of client loyalty, expansion, and a more prominent position in the market as your e-commerce business develops and expands.

4.2- Creating a compelling brand identity.

A strong brand identity is essential in today's market to attract new clients, retain existing ones, and set your company apart from the competition. Your brand's identity is comprised of more than simply your logo; it also includes the brand's values, tone of voice, and visual components. Learn the fundamentals of branding and get actionable advice for making your company's name a household name with this comprehensive book.

Reasons Why Your Brand's Image Is Crucial

1. Recognition: A distinct brand identity makes a company more visible and recognisable in a crowded market. Your logo and brand colours should evoke positive associations in the minds of your customers.

Two, it helps to keep your brand's message and values consistent throughout all of your marketing materials and customer interactions. Due to this reliability is increased.

3. Trust and Loyalty: Consumers are more inclined to trust and continue to be loyal to a brand with which they feel an emotional connection. When consumers form an emotional connection with a brand, they are more likely to remain loyal to that brand.

4. Differentiation: A distinct brand identity helps you stand out in a sea of competitors offering identical goods and services. What sets you apart from the competition and why customers should choose you are highlighted.

5. Brand Recall: Having a memorable brand identity helps consumers remember your company. Your brand should be the first thing that customers think of when they need a product or service in a certain category.

The Elements of a Strong Brand Name

Brand Mission and Brand Values: Create a brand mission and brand values statement. When people think of your company, what do they think of? This is the bedrock around which the rest of your brand's identity is built.

Second, "Brand Personality:" Identify your brand's character. How cordial, formal, humorous, or solemn is it? The tone of your brand should reflect the tastes of its intended consumers.

Determine your brand's Unique Selling Proposition (USP) and the benefits it offers over competitors. Unique selling proposition (USP) is a vital part of your company's image.

4. Visual Identity: This consists of your logo, colour scheme, typefaces, and images. All of these parts need to fit together to make a unified and appealing logo.
Fifth, establish the voice and tone that will be used while communicating about your brand. Do you prefer formality or informality? Humour or seriousness? Your tone of voice should be consistent with the character of your brand and appeal to your target demographic.

Create a memorable brand story that sticks with your customers. Tell your brand's story in a way that resonates with your audience emotionally by highlighting your company's beliefs and goals.

You may sum up your brand's core and unique selling proposition in a distinctive tagline or slogan, which brings us to number seven. It needs to get right to the point while also being memorable.

8. Customer Experience: The impression that customers form of your company is based on their total sum of interactions with it. Make

sure your website and customer service provide a uniform, pleasant experience for your customers.

9. Logo: Your logo is a visual representation of your brand, thus it should be created with those qualities in mind. A well-designed logo created by experts is money well spent.

Methods for Establishing a Memorable Brand

1. Audience Research: Investigate your audience thoroughly to learn about their likes, dislikes, habits, and requirements. Adjust your company's image so that it reflects their values.
2. Competitor Analysis: Examine the brand identities of your rivals to find weaknesses and openings. Make your brand memorable by catering to unfulfilled desires.

Keep your brand's identity straightforward and easy to understand at all times. Keep things simple to avoid overwhelming your customers. Simplicity increases recall.

Fourth, maintain uniformity in the way your brand's visual identity is used across all platforms. The reliability of a brand is bolstered by its constant representation.

Fifth, your brand's identity should adapt and develop over time as your company does. Maintain awareness of changes in the market and consumer tastes, and adapt your brand accordingly.

Illustrations of Powerful Brand Identities

1. Coca-Cola: The core values of the Coca-Cola brand are joy, optimism, and the sharing of good times with others. Its worldwide notoriety can be attributed in large part to the famous red logo and typography, which have stayed unchanged for decades.

The Apple brand is widely recognised as a symbol of cutting-edge technology, user-friendly products, and aesthetic brilliance. The brand's ideals and personality are reflected in the clean, simple logo and user-friendly goods.

Thirdly, we have Nike, whose brand values are based on the concepts of inspiration, determination, and athletic excellence. The "Just Do It" motto and the trademark swoosh design are intended to inspire customers to take action.

4. Tesla: Tesla's brand identity is founded on sustainability, innovative technology, and a drive to hasten the global transition to clean power. The sleek, contemporary branding and eco-friendly aesthetics of the product all speak to these ideals.

5. Disney: Disney's brand identity centres on the power of magic, creativity, and tales. The brand is beautiful and emotionally resonant because to the iconic logo and endearing characters.

Conclusion

An engaging brand identity is not a fixed idea, but rather an ever-evolving manifestation of your company's core beliefs, character traits, and point of difference in the marketplace. It's the assurance you give to your clientele and the bond you establish with them on a personal level. Developing a memorable brand name calls for in-depth knowledge of your intended market and a dedication to providing constant value.

Establishing your brand's goals, character traits, and visual components can help you create a name and face for your company that resonates with consumers. Don't forget that a strong brand identity may set you apart from the competition, earn the trust of your target audience, and encourage them to stick with you for the long haul. In the ever-changing corporate environment, nothing is more important than establishing a memorable brand identity.

4.3- Establishing brand trust and credibility.

Building trust and credibility is crucial for companies in today's highly competitive and digitally linked world. Customers' loyalty, spending habits, and the quality of long-term relationships are all influenced by a company's ability to earn and maintain their trust and credibility. The importance of trust and credibility in branding is discussed, as well as tactics for developing them and case studies of companies that have done so successfully.

The Value of Reliability and Authenticity in Branding

Customers will have faith in your business if they know they can trust you. Customers are more willing to try out a brand, spend money on its wares, and sing its praises to friends and family if they have faith in the company behind it.

2. Loyalty and Retention: The loyalty and retention rates of customers are better for a brand that they have faith in. Customers are more loyal to a brand they trust and are more inclined to make additional purchases.

3. Competitive Advantage: In oversaturated marketplaces, trust and reputation can give you a leg up on the competition. Customers are more inclined to choose a company over others if they have positive associations with the brand.

Risk reduction is achieved through the protective effects of credibility and trust in the face of adversity. Customers are more tolerant and understanding when a reputable company makes a mistake or encounters difficulties.

5. Brand Expansion: It is simpler for well-known brands to provide new products and services since consumers already know and like

them. Customers are more likely to test new products from well-known companies.

Methods for Building Reputation and Consumer Confidence in a Brand

First, always be consistent with your brand's voice and aesthetic. Keep your website, social media, and in-person encounters all consistent in terms of branding, messaging, and quality. Maintaining uniformity fosters trust.

Second, Transparency: Don't hide anything regarding your offerings or how you do business. Deliver precise and understandable details to your clients. Honesty and openness, which are exhibited by transparency, inspire confidence.

Third, keep your customers' wants and needs at the forefront of your mind. Pay attention to what they have to say, fix the things that bother them, and evolve as a result of their suggestions. A customer-focused strategy demonstrates respect for their thoughts and feelings.

4. Quality and Reliability: Always provide excellent workmanship. Keeping your word and following through on commitments will earn you respect and loyalty. Spend money on quality assurance to guarantee your products and services will satisfy your clients.

Fifth, use "social proof," such as reviews, testimonials, and case studies from satisfied customers. Social proof is the testimony of your delighted customers to the reliability and validity of your brand.

6. information Marketing: Produce information that is both useful and interesting to your target demographic. Create content that shows you put thought into what you're saying, and your brand will gain credibility as an industry leader.

7. Ethical Practises: Conduct all of your company dealings in an honest and upstanding manner. Don't engage in dishonest behaviour, and put morality first while making choices. Credibility and trust are developed by ethical actions.

Security Measures: Take all necessary precautions to safeguard sensitive customer information and data. Trust in e-commerce and other forms of online business relies heavily on the assurance of data security.

Brands that are widely recognised as trustworthy

First, there is Amazon, which has earned its customers' faith by consistently delivering on their expectations. Amazon has become a go-to internet retailer thanks to its prompt shipping, honest product reviews, and helpful staff.

Google's search engine is relied on by billions of people around the world because it always returns relevant results. The company's dedication to customer confidentiality has helped establish its reputation.

Third, Coca-Cola; for well over a hundred years, this soft drink has been a reliable option. The reliability of its offerings and the positivity of its marketing have earned the brand long-term confidence and trust.

When it comes to quality and dependability, few brands are as well-known as Toyota. Because of the company's dedication to safety and technological advancement, consumers have faith in their vehicles.

5. Apple: Apple's enduring popularity stems from the company's dedication to the security and privacy of its customers' personal

information when using its products. Its ecosystem and goods have earned the trust of the company's devoted clientele.

Conclusion

In the realm of branding, trust and credibility are priceless commodities. To achieve them, you must consistently put the needs of your customers first, provide them with excellent products or services, and be honest and trustworthy. Brands that are able to earn consumers' confidence and credibility are better able to win over new ones, keep existing ones, and thrive through adversity.

It's important to keep in mind that efforts to build your brand's trustworthiness and credibility are never finished. Customers will have faith in your brand if you consistently meet their expectations, act in an honest and ethical manner, and value their feedback. Building trust and credibility in a world when options are plentiful can lead to long-term success and devoted customers.

Chapter 5:
Marketing Methods in the Digital Age

5.1- Search Engine Optimization (SEO) techniques.

Optimising a website for search engines like Google, Bing, and Yahoo is known as search engine optimisation (SEO). Search engine optimisation (SEO) is the process of enhancing a website's visibility in search engine results without paying for that visibility or those results. This tutorial will help you improve your website's search engine rankings and overall performance by exploring numerous SEO approaches, strategies, and best practises.

First, an Examination of Keywords

Doing extensive keyword research is the first step to effective SEO. Users of search engines use what are called "keywords" to help narrow their results. Your website can be optimised for certain keywords if you know which ones are both relevant to your business and receive a lot of monthly searches. How to conduct keyword research:

Find appropriate terms with the use of keyword research tools like Google's Keyword Planner, SEMrush, Ahrefs, or Moz's Keyword Explorer.
- Use both broad and long-tail keywords (particular phrases).
Identify profitable keyword opportunities by analysing competition and search traffic.
Think about what people are actually trying to find when they type a query into a search engine.

The Optimisation of On-Page SEO

Increasing a website's visibility in search results using on-page SEO. Some of the most important parts of on-page optimisation are:

Create engaging and informative title tags that include relevant keywords for each page. Titles should be short, usually no more than 70 characters.

Create engaging meta descriptions (no more than 160 characters) that incorporate keywords and increase click-throughs.

Use header tags (H1, H2, H3, etc.) to organise and highlight important sections of text for your readers. Wherever possible, use headers with keyword phrases.

- Keyword Optimisation: Use your target keywords in the first paragraph, headings, and body text in a natural way.

Optimise photos by giving them meaningful titles and include keyword-rich alt text.

Create URLs that are easy to read, explain the page's content, and use relevant keywords. This is the URL Structure.

To better facilitate site navigation and share link equity, consider implementing an internal linking strategy.

Google now takes into account a site's mobile-friendliness when determining its search engine rankings, so it's important to make sure your site is optimised for mobile users.

To improve website load times, use image compression, browser caching, and as few HTTP queries as possible.

3. Quality and Pertinence of Content

The success of an SEO strategy relies heavily on fresh, relevant content. Content that is useful to users is given higher rankings in search results. Think about these suggestions:

To reach your audience, you need to produce material that is both unique and interesting.

Duplicate material can hurt your search engine rankings, so try to avoid it. To designate preferred versions of pages with comparable content, use canonical tags.

Updating information regularly is essential. Keep your readers interested by updating or publishing new content on a consistent basis.
Improve the user experience with the help of visual and auditory media as well as interactive features.

4. Off-Page SEO and Backlinks

Inbound links, also known as backlinks, are links on other websites that lead back to yours. Backlinks are an indicator of your site's authority and relevance to search engines. To strengthen your link profile, try these steps:

Build authoritative backlinks by producing content that others will want to share.
Get in touch with bloggers and thought leaders in your field and ask them to share your content and link to it.
- Building authority and links at the same time by contributing as a guest blogger on related sites.
- Keep an eye on your backlink profile with the help of software like Ahrefs or Moz so you can disavow any low-quality or potentially damaging connections.

5. SEO Techniques

Improving your site's performance and crawlability for search engines is a goal of technical SEO. Important technical SEO methods consist of:

- Site Speed: Reduce HTTP requests, compress pictures, and use a content delivery network (CDN) to improve website load times.
Mobile optimisation is making sure your site displays properly across all mobile devices.
If you want search engines to better index your site's content, you should make an XML sitemap and submit it to them.

Use a file called robots.txt to specify which parts of your site search engines should and should not index.
When there are many versions of a page, use canonical tags to indicate which one should be prioritised.
Secure your site with an SSL certificate to protect user information and improve search engine rankings.

UX 6: The User's Perspective

Positive UX is critical for search engine optimisation. Bounce rate, dwell time, and click-through rate are all metrics used by search engines to gauge the experience of their users. If you want to enhance user experience:

Make sure your website has well-organized menus and material that is easy to find.
Make use of mobile-friendly features by employing responsive design.
Improve user retention by decreasing page load times.
Design simple, straightforward, and intuitive forms and buttons.
User testing and feedback collection is essential for locating and fixing usability problems.

7. Local Search Engine Optimisation

Local search engine optimisation is crucial for brick and mortar businesses. It increases your visibility in "near me" and other location-based search engine results. Examples of essential local SEO strategies include:

Take control of your online presence by claiming and populating your Google My Business (GMB) page with relevant data.
Make sure to respond quickly and positively to customer feedback.
Put your company's information in as many relevant online directories and websites as possible.

Include geo-targeted search terms in your articles' titles, summaries, and body text.

Analysing and Keeping Tabs on Things

Consistently checking in on your SEO efforts and analysing the outcomes will allow you to make educated selections. Important KPIs to monitor:

- Organic traffic: Keep an eye on how many people are finding you through natural search results.
Monitor where you stand in relation to competing pages for specific keywords.
Find out how many people really click on your search results by calculating the click-through rate (CTR).
Examine the percentage of site visitors who do the intended action (placing a purchase, for example, or submitting a contact form) by using the "conversion rate" metric.
Calculate the percentage of visitors that only read one page before leaving your site (the "bounce rate").

Conclusion

Because of this constant flux, SEO experts must constantly monitor the latest algorithm updates and industry developments. If you want to improve your website's visibility in search engines, increase your organic traffic, and eventually reach your digital marketing goals, then you need to implement these SEO strategies and best practises. As a business owner, marketer, or website administrator, your long-term online success depends on your ability to keep up with SEO trends and invest resources into optimisation.

5.2- Social media marketing strategies.

Connection, promotion, and brand recognition for businesses have all been revolutionised by the advent of social media. To compete successfully and reach today's technologically sophisticated consumers, businesses need to implement efficient social media marketing tactics. In this all-inclusive guide, you'll learn about the most effective ways to market your business on social media, as well as see real-world case studies of companies that have used these tactics to great effect.

Why Social Media Marketing Is Crucial

For many good reasons, social media sites are become an essential part of today's marketing mix:

1. Massive Audience: With billions of monthly active users, social media platforms offer businesses access to a large and varied audience.

2. Targeted Marketing: Modern targeting tools let companies zero in on very precise audiences based on their demographics, interests, and behaviours.

Thirdly, Brand Visibility is improved by an active social media presence, making it simpler for consumers to find and interact with a brand.
Relationship-building and customer-engagement are facilitated by the direct and real-time communication made possible by social media.

Fifthly, it is an effective means of disseminating content such as articles, movies, infographics, and advertisements.

Sixthly, Data and Insights: Social Media platforms offer insightful data and analytics that may be used to gauge the success of advertising campaigns and guide company decisions.

Promoting Your Business Through Social Media

Determine what you want and write it down Get started with your social media marketing by establishing clear objectives. Brand recognition, site visits, new leads, and revenue growth are all common targets.

2. Know Your Audience: Be aware of the demographics, interests, pain areas, and behaviours of your intended audience. Your content and messaging strategies will benefit from this insight.

Thirdly, Content Strategy and Development: Create a content plan that caters to the needs and interests of your target demographic. Make use of a content schedule to keep your updates varied and regular.

4. Pick the Right Platforms: Not every social media site is a good fit for every company. You should pick channels that are appropriate for reaching your intended demographic. For instance, LinkedIn may be a better fit for business-to-business operations, whereas aesthetic enterprises may find success on Instagram.

Content Variety is the fifth way to keep your audience interested and involved. Disseminate a wide range of media, including but not limited to text, graphics, audio, and video.

Engagement and Interaction 6: Get back to people quickly when they leave comments, send messages, or mention you. Polls, surveys, and contests are great ways to interact with your audience and encourage user-generated content.

Consistency in blogging is crucial to retaining readers and viewers. Plan and automate your posts with the help of scheduling tools.

Use media such as photos and videos to tell interesting tales about your company in 8. In general, social media users respond well to visual content.

Paid Social media advertising should be considered for allocation of funds. Social media sites like Facebook and Instagram let you zero in on your ideal customers with pinpoint accuracy.

10Influencer Marketing: Work with popular people in your field to gain exposure to their fans and customers. Make sure the influencer's beliefs are consistent with those of your company. Eleven. Hashtags: Make your material more searchable by including current and popular hashtags. But choose your hashtags carefully and don't stuff your postings with them.

Analyse your social media performance on a regular basis utilising the analytics tools provided by each platform as well as external analytics software. Make strategic changes in light of new information.

Guidelines for Successful Social Media Marketing

First, authenticity, always be yourself when interacting with others online. Being genuine increases your audience's confidence in you.

2. Consistent Branding: Use the same profile picture, cover photo, and voice on all of your social media channels.

Third, remember that your business exists to serve your customers, so always have their demands and issues front and centre. Focus your social media efforts on ensuring the happiness of your customers.

Fourth, provide a fast response to all client complaints and questions. Responding quickly demonstrates that you appreciate your audience's time and thoughts.

5. A/B Testing: Try out various content types, publishing timings, and ad formats to see what your target audience responds to best. Sharing helpful and educational material that establishes your brand as an authority in its field is tip number six. The audience can be both entertained and informed by writing how-to guides, tutorials, and educational articles.

Marketing Strategies That Worked Well on Social Media

1. Nike: Nike's social media approach centres on encouraging and energising its target demographic to reach for the stars in all forms of athletic competition. They are constant contributors to social media sites like Instagram, where they provide inspirational quotes, athlete profiles, and visually amazing imagery.

The second example is Wendy's, which has become well-known for its creative and amusing Twitter presence. There is a sizable and vocal fan base for this method.

Thirdly, Dove, whose "Real Beauty" social media campaign debunks unrealistic beauty standards and encourages body acceptance. Their meaningful messages hit home with their intended listeners and spark conversations about self-love and acceptance.

GoPro, number four: GoPro features user-created content to promote their action cameras. Customers are effectively turned into brand ambassadors as they are encouraged to share their exciting excursions and breathtaking footage.

5. Airbnb: The Instagram page for Airbnb is a treasure trove of beautiful travel photos and user-created content from all around the

world's most interesting lodgings. Their stories in pictures make you want to travel and advertise their service.

Conclusion

Keeping abreast of the latest developments and best practises in the dynamic realm of social media marketing is essential. A great social media presence that generates brand awareness, engagement, and conversions is the result of deliberate planning, in-depth research into your target demographic, the production of high-quality content, and the maintenance of an honest demeanour in all of your interactions. The goal of modern digital marketing should be to engage with your target audience and create a mutually beneficial connection with them.

5.3- Email marketing campaigns.

As a form of digital marketing, email marketing is both flexible and effective. Businesses can now reach out to customers on a more personal level, nurture leads, and increase sales with the help of this tool. Learn everything you need to know about effective email marketing campaigns, from goal-setting and list-building to content creation and analytics, with this in-depth book.

The Importance of Electronic Mail Marketing

There are several good reasons why email marketing is still so important in the digital marketing world.

The primary benefit of email is that it enables businesses to have one-on-one conversations with their customers by sending them messages directly to their inboxes.

2. Cost-Effective: It is a marketing strategy that, if done properly, can generate a significant return on investment (ROI).

Thirdly, emails can be customised to each recipient based on their interests and past actions, a feature made possible by email marketing.
4. Targeting: Businesses can divide their email lists into smaller subsets and send more relevant and engaging messages to those subsets.
5. Automation: Automation technologies enable the development of automated email workflows that nurture leads and direct them towards the closing of a deal.

Sixthly, Measurable Results: Businesses can easily monitor metrics like email campaign open rates, click-through rates, conversion rates, and more with email marketing campaigns.

Preparing for an Email Marketing Effort

It is crucial to properly plan an email marketing strategy before going headfirst into its execution:

1. Establish Your Goals: To begin, your campaign has to have defined goals. The most common objectives are to increase site visits, leads, sales, and brand recognition.

2. Know Who You're Talking To: Get to know your intended market very well. Develop in-depth buyer personas to identify with potential customers and learn about their wants, needs, and buying habits.

Third, compile a solid list of email addresses for your subscriber base. Create a list of people who have opted in to receiving your emails by asking for their information.

4. Divide and conquer: categorise your subscribers into distinct groups based on their interests, demographics, and previous purchases. Targeted communications are made possible by segmentation.

5. Create Intriguing Content: Write about topics that are of interest to your target market. Content, whether an informative piece, a promotional offer, or a newsletter, must be useful.

Select an Email Marketing Platform that Meets Your Requirements (Step 6). SendinBlue, HubSpot, SendChimp, and ConstantContact are some of the most well-known choices.

The subject line is the first thing that your receivers will see, therefore it's important to make it interesting. Use a captivating subject line to get people to open your email.

Since a large percentage of email opens occur on mobile devices, it's important to design emails that are mobile-responsive. Create designs that are neat and aesthetically pleasing.

To get the most out of your email marketing, you need to do some A/B testing. Try sending at various times and experimenting with different subject lines and content types.

Depending on where your audience is located, you may need to adhere to different email marketing legislation such as the CAN-SPAM Act or the General Data Protection Regulation (GDPR).

Putting Your Email Marketing Strategy Into Action
Now that you have your strategy in place, let's talk about putting it into action:

1. Select the Appropriate Email Format:

   - Advertising Emails: Spread the word about your company's latest deals, sales, and goods.
   Transactional emails include things like order confirmations, receipts, and updates on the status of such orders.
   Send out emails that provide educational resources like webinars, ebooks, and blog entries.
   - Welcome Emails: Hello and Introduce your brand to new subscribers.
   Send emails to customers who have abandoned their shopping carts, reminding them of the products they were planning to buy but never got around to.
   Win back dormant subscribers with Re-engagement Emails by providing them with special offers or content.

Second, employ personalization techniques like greeting people by name and sending them content that is tailored to their specific interests and habits.

Third, make sure your material is compelling and interesting to the people who will be reading it. Make your call to action (CTA) explicit and use convincing language.

4. Timing: Test out different sending windows to see when your audience engages the most. What time is best might vary depending on a number of factors, including time zone and the specifics of your material.

5. Design Make sure it looks nice and is easy on the eyes. If you want your emails to be read and navigated on mobile devices, you need to make sure they are.

6. A/B Testing: Run A/B testing on various parts to see what connects with your audience, such as subject lines, CTAs, email copy, and visuals.

7. Automation: Make use of automated email sequences for tasks like lead nurturing, onboarding, and post-purchase communication.

Over 50% of email opens now occur on mobile devices, thus it's important to 8. optimise for mobile. Make sure your emails are compatible with mobile devices.

Use analytics and tracking tools to assess the efficacy of your email marketing initiatives. Keep an eye on your email's open, click, conversion, and unsubscribe rates to gauge its efficacy.

Ten. Constantly analyse and refine your campaign based on your findings through monitoring and iteration. Improve the success of future efforts by applying what you've learned.
Assessing the Performance of Your Email Marketing Effort

The success of your email marketing strategy may be gauged by keeping tabs on the right metrics and KPIs. Some very important indicators to keep an eye on are:

The fraction of people that actually bothered to open your email (the "Open Rate").
CTR stands for the number of people who opened your email and went on to click on a link contained therein.
Conversion rate is the proportion of people who take the intended action after being presented with an offer (buying something, submitting a form, etc.).
Undeliverable email volume is measured by the Bounce Rate.
- Unsubscribe Rate: The amount of people that decided to be removed from your email distribution list.
The rate at which your email list is expanding over time is referred to as the "List Growth Rate."
The sum of money you made thanks to your email marketing efforts; also known as "Revenue Generated."

Successful Email Marketing Efforts as Examples

First, Airbnb's emails are both visually appealing and individually tailored to each user. They deliver personalised messages to each user with suggestions based on their previous searches, ticket confirmations, and travel ideas.
Spotify offers consumers customised email campaigns that highlight their listening patterns, such as the songs and artists they listen to the most. This method fosters a feeling of community and individualization.

Thirdly, Grammarly provides readers with helpful weekly reports that detail their writing progress, productivity, and vocabulary usage. The emails stress the importance of consistent platform use.

The Dropbox referral programme rewards users who invite their friends and coworkers to use Dropbox. The emails they send out in exchange for referrals are easy to understand and provide value to the referrer as well as the user they're trying to attract.

Reebok's abandoned cart emails feature eye-catching images of the things the customer nearly bought but didn't, alluring price cuts, and prominent calls to action.

Conclusion

Email marketing campaigns are still an effective method of connecting with customers, increasing sales, and reaching business objectives. Businesses may take use of email marketing to build meaningful relationships with their target audiences with proper strategy, creation of attractive content, execution, and measurement of outcomes. Staying in sync with your audience's wants and requirements is essential to long-term success in the digital era, so keep in mind that perfecting your email marketing is an ongoing process.

5.4- Paid advertising and conversion optimization.

Paid advertising is a crucial part of digital marketing since it allows brands to directly communicate with their target demographic and generate more leads. However, it is not enough to merely display advertisements; conversion optimisation of your campaigns is also essential. This article will help you maximise your advertising dollars and advance your business goals by exploring paid advertising strategies and conversion optimisation methods.

The Importance of Sponsored Content

Several persuasive arguments support the importance of paid advertising in contemporary digital marketing:

First, Immediate Visibility: Paid advertising give companies instantaneous exposure on search engines and social media platforms, allowing them to contact potential customers at the optimal time.

Ads are shown to the most relevant audience thanks to advanced targeting tools that allow businesses to target certain demographics, interests, and behaviours.

Third, paid advertising programmes can be expanded or contracted according to their success and available funds.

Fourth, Measurable Results: Advertising Platforms offer powerful analytics, allowing organisations to monitor KPIs and make decisions based on hard data.

5. Competitive Edge: Paid advertising can give organisations an edge in highly competitive markets.

Promoting Methods That Cost Money

Careful planning, strategy, and execution are essential for successful paid advertising initiatives. Key approaches include the following:

1. Establish Your Goals: Get started with your paid advertising efforts by establishing crystal-clear and -specific objectives. Goals including expanding audience reach, attracting new customers, boosting revenue, and popularising a brand are typical.

Pick the Best Advertising Medium

   Google advertising are perfect for SEM because they are text advertising that show up in search engine results.
   Ads on Facebook, for example, let you narrow in on a certain audience based on their demographics and interests.
   LinkedIn ads are a good fit for business-to-business (B2B) campaigns since they provide specific targeting by occupation and industry.
   Instagram Ads is a photo and video sharing app that caters to visually appealing marketers.
   Promote trends, tweets, and brand recognition with Twitter Ads.
   Advertisements that can be skipped or not on YouTube are called YouTube Ads.

Third, you need to do some keyword research to find out what people are actually typing into search engines. Finding valuable keywords might be difficult, but tools like Google's Keyword Planner can help.

Ad language and imagery should be captivating and resonant with the intended audience. Include a compelling call to action (CTA) and make your point(s) clear.

5. Landing Page Optimisation: Make sure the page your advertising direct people to converts as well as it could. A good CTA is one that is relevant to the ad, loads quickly, and is easy to understand.

Consider the platform, campaign goals, and target demographic when allocating your advertising budget. Spending should be tracked and adjusted as necessary.

Seventh, schedule your ads to appear when your target audience is most likely to see them.

Using ad extensions, you may add more information to your ads and boost their visibility. Links to external websites, in-text citations, and code snippets are all possible additions.

9. Remarketing: Run campaigns aimed at people who have visited your website before but not converted. Lead nurturing via remarketing is a powerful tool.

Methods for Improving Conversion Rates

You must optimise your website or landing page for conversions once you have garnered visitors through paid advertising. Some essential methods are as follows:

Value Proposition That Is Both Specific and Enticing Explain to them how your product or service is superior than others. Emphasise the positives and the answers to their issues.

Conversion Paths that Are Easier to Navigate Make the process of converting as easy and painless as possible. Reduce resistance by performing tasks in as few steps as possible.

3. A/B Testing: Try out multiple variations of features including headlines, graphics, calls to action, and form fields to see which ones result in higher conversion rates.

Optimise your website and landing pages for mobile devices so that they load quickly and provide a pleasant experience for mobile visitors.

Fifthly, use social proof like reviews, testimonials, and trust badges from satisfied customers to bolster your brand's trustworthiness. Individualise each user's experience by catering to their unique tastes and habits with the use of dynamic content and personalisation (see point 6).

7. Exit-Intent Popups: Use them to gather contact information from visitors who are about to leave your site. Obtain their information by offering incentives or exclusive content.

Eighth, boost your site's loading speed; users are less likely to stick around if pages take too long to load.

Use 9: Trust Signals to convince site visitors that their information is safe by showcasing things like SSL certificates, secure payment icons, and privacy policy links.

10 Analytics and Insights: Always keep an eye on your website's analytics to keep tabs on user behaviour and find out where you can make changes. Take advantage of heatmaps and recorded user sessions to learn more about how users engage with your site.

Case Studies in Paid Promotion and Conversion Enhancement

One example is Amazon, which does a great job of integrating paid advertising with conversion optimisation strategies. High conversion rates are achieved by curated product listings, persuasive ad language, and a quick purchasing procedure.

2. HubSpot: HubSpot's marketing automation software is the primary focus of their paid advertising initiatives. They deploy persuasive ad language, landing sites with obvious calls to action, and A/B testing to maximise clickthroughs.

Thirdly, Shopify: Shopify uses sponsored advertising to entice online retailers. In order to increase conversions, they deploy landing pages that emphasise the platform's simplicity, provide free trials, and feature customer success stories.

Fourth, Netflix: Netflix promotes its content to a global audience through sponsored advertising. In order to increase conversions, their landing pages feature tailored suggestions and prominent calls to action for signing up.

In order to maximise the effectiveness of its paid advertisements, LinkedIn uses a combination of advanced targeting and conversion optimisation strategies. They advertise webinars, eBooks, and other content with clear value propositions that leads to lead generation forms.

Conclusion
In digital marketing, paid advertising and conversion optimisation are like two sides of the same coin. The goal of conversion optimisation is to increase the percentage of visitors that take some sort of action on your site, such as subscribing, buying something, or contacting you. You may increase your marketing return on investment (ROI), as well as accomplish your business goals, by learning about your target market, making engaging advertisements, and continuously optimising your conversion paths. It's an ever-evolving process that calls for a focus on the smallest of details, a willingness to try new things, and a dedication to provide an outstanding user experience.

Chapter 6:
Interaction With Users And The Customer Experience

6.1- Designing a user-friendly online shopping experience.

Online buying has grown increasingly common in modern society. Shopping has been completely transformed by e-commerce platforms, which provide us with ease, variety, and availability. However, an online shop's ability to attract customers depends on how easy it is to use. In this detailed tutorial, we'll look at what it takes to create a shopping portal that not only draws in new customers but also keeps them coming back for more.

The Importance of a User-Friendly Interface

Having a storefront that is easy on the eyes is crucial to the success of any online business. The reason it does is because:

1. Customer Satisfaction: Customers are more likely to return and be loyal if they have a positive buying experience.

2. Conversion Rate: An user-friendly interface can increase conversion rates by converting site visitors into paying clients.
3. Decreased Bounce Rate: Visitors to user-friendly sites are more likely to stick around, investigate further, and make a purchase.
4. Competitive Advantage: In today's crowded e-commerce market, having a website that is easy to navigate will give your company a leg up on the competition.

5. Mobile Responsiveness: With the rise of mobile internet purchasing, a responsive design is essential to providing a good experience across all devices.

Guiding Principles for Creating a Pleasant Online Shopping Experience

First, Intuitive Browsing:

Make it simple for visitors to find what they're looking for by using well-organized menus that convey relevant information.
Access to a Search Engine: Create a powerful search bar that offers a variety of filters, sorting options, and auto-suggestions.
Breadcrumb trails should be provided so that users can see where they are in relation to the rest of the site.

Product Development That Gets Results

- Featured Products: Feature new or best-selling products prominently on the site.
Make sure your category thumbnails are easy on the eyes and contain only the most essential information.
- Filtering and Sorting: Let shoppers narrow down results by selecting certain attributes like price, brand, size, and colour.

Easy-to-navigate product pages (3):

Include high-resolution photographs from a variety of perspectives, a zoom feature, and galleries of individual images.
Include all relevant information, such as features, benefits, and technical specs, in your product descriptions.
Please be as transparent as possible with price, special offers, and stock levels.
Include user-generated reviews and ratings to inspire confidence and facilitate choice.

Quick and Easy Checkout:

- One-Page Checkout: Reduce the number of pages needed for the purchase procedure to a minimum.

To facilitate purchases without requiring customers to sign up for an account, we offer a guest checkout option.

Provide a selection of several ways to pay, such as different credit card options, digital wallets, and layaway plans.

Fifth, "Responsive Design":

Make sure your site responds to the size of the screen it's being viewed on.

To guarantee a uniform experience across browsers and devices, you should conduct extensive testing.

Sixthly, Security and Trust:

To reassure users that their information is secure, you should feature trust badges, security seals, and SSL certifications.

Make sure your terms of service and privacy policies are easy to understand.

7. Speed of Loading:

Minimise lost visitors by making your website load quickly. Reduce the number of HTTP requests by compressing pictures and use browser caching.

Easy-to-navigate shopping bag and wish list 8

Facilitate the process of adding and removing goods from one's shopping cart and wish list.

Highlight the items in the shopping basket and their total price so that customers can easily continue to the checkout page.

Powerful Search Capabilities, 9.

Build a site search that is both fast and accurate.

Help customers find what they're looking for with auto-suggestions and predictive search.

Optimisation for Mobile, No. 10:

- Give mobile optimisation top priority to make mobile purchasing as painless as possible.
Make sure the menus, buttons, and forms are all mobile-friendly.

Eleventhly, Unmistakable CTAs:

Take advantage of prominent calls to action (CTAs) like "Add to Cart," "Buy Now," and "Checkout" to increase conversions.
Keep your website's call-to-action buttons looking the same.

Guidelines for an Optimal Digital Storefront Design

First, Streamline Registration by letting users join up with as little detail as possible and providing options to sign up using existing social media profiles.

Second, Progress Indicators should be made available to customers so they know how far along in the checkout process they are. Provide immediate assistance to customers via chat, email, or phone if they have any concerns or inquiries.

Make sure your customers understand your return and refund policies so they feel comfortable making purchases from you.

Use a distinct visual hierarchy to highlight important details like product photos, prices, and calls to action.

6. Optimised photographs and Videos: Make sure the photographs and videos of your products load quickly and accurately portray the products they depict.

7. Cross-Selling and Upselling: Recommend complementary products or accessories on product pages and in the cart to increase the likelihood of a sale.

Use loading animations to let users know you're working on their request, such as when they're adding an item to their shopping cart.

9. User Testing: Run usability tests with actual visitors to your site to learn about their experiences and where you can make improvements.

Instances of Pleasant Online Shopping

First, there's Amazon, whose layout makes it easy to find what you're looking for thanks to its organised menus, quick search bar, and comprehensive product pages that feature high-resolution photographs and customer reviews.

Zappo's, Number Two: Zappos

 puts the needs of its customers first by providing them with a straightforward interface, superior search functionality, and a liberal return policy.

Thirdly, Apple: Shopping on Apple's website is a pleasant and streamlined experience because to the clear layout, short descriptions, and user-friendly interface.

ASOS, the fourth on our list, offers a visually appealing shopping experience with high-quality photographs and videos, in-depth product descriptions, and a mobile-friendly design.

5 Etsy: Etsy's user-friendly platform provides a personalised shopping feed, easy-to-navigate categories, and a powerful search option for locating one-of-a-kind, handcrafted items.

Conclusion

In today's increasingly competitive e-commerce industry, creating a user-friendly online shopping experience is crucial to attracting and maintaining customers. Businesses can establish an atmosphere where customers feel safe and confident making purchases by following to principles of easy navigation, quick product discovery, responsive design, and trust-building measures. Maintaining leadership in the competitive world of e-commerce requires routinely evaluating and updating your website's design in light of user feedback and new best practises. Keep in mind that a happy consumer is much more likely to become a repeat buyer, which is the key to the sustainable growth of your e-commerce company.

6.2- Enhancing the customer journey.

Providing an amazing client journey is no longer a luxury in today's highly competitive company world. When customers have a good experience, it's good for business in the long run since they're more likely to recommend your brand to others. To keep customers coming back, it's important to provide them with memorable and fulfilling experiences along their trip, and this guide will cover the ideas and tactics for doing just that.

Recognising the Customer's Perspective

The customer journey encompasses the entire time a client interacts with your company, from the moment they become aware of you until long after they have made a purchase. It includes a wide range of encounters, such as those with the company's website, its physical stores, its customer support department, and so on. To make this trip better, knowledge is power.

First, customers need to become aware of your brand, product, or service before they can make a purchase.

2. Consideration: The buyer thinks about what you're selling and how it stacks up against other options.

3. Purchase: The buyer makes up their mind to buy and finalises the deal.
A customer's engagement with your brand begins with their post-purchase evaluation of their experience.

Why Should We Improve the Customer Experience

It's win-win when businesses and customers work together to improve the customer experience:

1. consumer Loyalty: A satisfied consumer is less likely to defect to a rival if their experience has been a good one.

2. More Money: Loyal buyers tend to spend more money and buy more frequently.

Third, "word of mouth," or recommendations from happy consumers to their friends and family.

The competitive edge that comes from providing an exceptional customer journey is substantial.

Five, Feedback and Improvement: Throughout the journey, customer feedback provides insights that can be used to make changes for the better.

Guidelines for Improving the Customer Experience
Use these guidelines to design a customer experience that will wow your target market.

The Customer-Centric Methodology

   The consumer should always come first in any business's decision-making.
   Research and feedback from customers can help you learn about their wants, needs, and problem points.

2 Consistency in All Interactions:

   Maintain cohesion throughout your brand's digital, in-store, and customer service interactions.
   Keep consistent brand voice, messaging, and imagery.

Third, a Integrated Omnichannel Flow:

Allow customers to easily switch from one channel to another (such as online to in-store) without any hiccups in service, and provide a consistent experience across all channels and platforms.

Tailoring and individualization:
   - Cater your interactions, suggestions, and products to each individual customer's tastes and habits.
   Make use of digital tools and data to provide custom service.

5. Compassion and Insight:

   Consider the customer's perspective and feelings, especially in trying circumstances.
   Demonstrate that you get the situation and are eager to work through it.

Sixthly, Unambiguous Expression:

   Maintain open lines of communication throughout the trip.
   Avoid complicated terminology and provide as much detail as possible.

Speed and ease of use:

   Reduce friction and increase efficiency to help clients get what they want as soon as possible.
   Reduce any obstacles or hassles that can put off potential buyers.

Strategies for Improving the Customer Experience

One, Depict the Customer Flow:
   Construct a comprehensive diagram of the customer's experience, including all points of contact.
   Find out where your clients are having difficulty, where there is room for growth, and when it really matters to them.

2. Spend Money on Professional Development:

Educate workers on how to better interact with customers and one another.
- Promote internal organisational values that place emphasis on serving customers.

Use Technology to Your Advantage

- Use customer relationship management (CRM) software to keep tabs on communications and tailor offerings to each individual client.
Automated customer service through the use of chatbots and other AI-enabled solutions.

4. Solicit and respond to comments:

Encourage comments and suggestions via surveys, reviews, and support chats.
Examine comments for patterns and room for development.
5. Tailor Ads and Recommendations to Each Individual:
Make your marketing and product suggestions more relevant by digging into the numbers.
Distribute targeted advertisements and articles to customers.

Sixth, Enable Patrons:

Make it possible for customers to get answers on their own with the help of self-service tools like FAQs and knowledge bases.
Allow consumers to view order status updates, make account adjustments, and set personal preferences.

Brand Consistency:

Keep the look, feel, and values of your brand consistent at all times.

Maintain uniformity of presentation across all mediums.

8. Preemptive Assistance:

Predict what the customer will want and give it to them before they ever ask.

Proactively offer assistance and answers in times of need.

Thank You, Customers, No. 9:

Customers should be thanked for their continued patronage through special promotions, price reductions, or handwritten notes of appreciation.

- Recognise significant moments for your customers, such as anniversaries or advancements in a loyalty programme.

Outstanding Customer Journey Examples

Amazon: 1.

Amazon's customer service is second to none due to the company's attention to detail and the ease with which customers may buy from any of their devices.

Zappos, 2:

Zappos is well-known for its high-quality customer care, which includes a convenient return policy and round-the-clock help. One of the company's defining characteristics is its dedication to customer happiness.

Thirdly, Disney Theme Parks:

The Disney parks provide visitors with an enchanting and exciting experience. Everything, from the themed attractions to the character encounters, is made to leave guests with lifelong smiles and fond recollections.

4. Apple:

The Apple customer experience is built around ease of use, compatibility, and a unified ecosystem. Customers are more satisfied when they are able to easily transition between their internet research and their in-store encounters.

JetBlue, number 5.

JetBlue's customer service is notable for its warmth and openness. It's known for its helpful staff, in-flight entertainment, and proactive flight status updates.

Conclusion

Improving the customer experience is something that should be done constantly with care, compassion, and a focus on the customer's wants and needs. Creating outstanding experiences that not only please customers but also inspire loyalty and advocacy requires putting the customer first, using technology in a smart manner, and continuously refining your approach based on feedback and data. The customer journey is an investment in the future of your company in an era where customer experience is a key difference.

6.3- Strategies for improving user interface and navigation.

The layout and ease of use of a digital product's user interface (UI) and navigational system are of paramount importance. Improved user engagement, retention, and happiness can be the consequence of an interface that is both easy to use and straightforward to navigate. In this detailed manual, we will examine methods and recommendations for enhancing user interface and navigation to provide users with a superior digital experience.

User Experience Design and Navigation.

The importance of user interface and navigation should not be underestimated before diving into potential solutions.

The user interface (UI) is the very first thing that people see when they engage with your digital product. An intuitive and aesthetically pleasing user interface is more likely to be used.

2. Usability: A user-friendly interface and navigation system make it simple for customers to learn how to utilise your product.

User Retention, or the percentage of customers that decide to keep using your product after their initial trial period.
Fourthly, Conversion Rates: If the user interface and navigation of an e-commerce website or app are well-designed, the number of people who actually make a purchase is likely to increase.
5. Competitive Advantage: In today's crowded digital market, your product can stand out from the crowd with an exceptional user interface and straightforward navigation.

Strategies for Enhancing the User Experience

1) Get to Know Your Audience:

User research is a great way to learn more about your intended audience's wants, tastes, and problems.
- Figure out who your usual customers are by developing user personas.

2. De-Clutter the User Interface:

Adopt a minimalistic approach by doing away with extraneous features and widgets in the user interface.
Content and features that help users achieve their top priorities should be given top billing.

Thirdly, Give Mobile Responsiveness Top Priority:

Make sure your user interface (UI) is mobile-friendly by optimising it for different screen widths.
Make sure your user interface is compatible with a wide range of browsers and hardware.

Unambiguous and Reliable Visual Presentation:

Guide users' focus to the most crucial parts of each screen by employing a distinct visual hierarchy.
Don't change the colours, fonts, or layout of your goods anywhere.

Friendly Typography (No. 5):

Make sure the fonts and sizes you use are legible.
Make sure there is enough white space between lines and that the text stands out against the background.

Intuitive Navigation, Number Six:

Use simple menu structures and hierarchies for navigation.

Label and/or use icons for navigation components that are easily understood.

Sticky menus and navigation bars can let consumers quickly access frequently used features of your product.

7. Confirmation and Feedback:

Give instant responses to user inputs like button presses and form submissions.

Provide users with affirmation messages after they've completed important tasks to give them peace of mind.

User Testing, number 8.

Use real people in usability tests to learn where your interface and navigation could use improvement.

Refine your product based on the results of usability tests.

9. Incremental Disclosing:

Display data in a sequential fashion, revealing only the required pieces at each stage.

Make use of accordion or extensible blocks to bury or unveil more details.

Accessible Design, Number 10.

Make sure that users with disabilities may easily use your interface and menus. Some examples of this are captions for photographs, links for the visually impaired, and clear labels for input fields.

Elements That Can Be Interacted With 11

Make use of sliders, toggles, and other interactive components to keep your users interested.

Make sure the interactive parts are simple to use and offer helpful feedback.

Search Capabilities:

Create a powerful search function that helps users locate information rapidly.
Offer filters and autocomplete recommendations to narrow search results.

B-Testing, or 13.

Determine which versions of the user interface and navigation structures lead to the highest levels of user engagement and highest conversion rates by running A/B tests.

Loading times 14

Reduce load times by improving your product's performance. If it takes too long for a product to load, users will become disinterested and leave.

15 Organising the Content:
- Make it easy for consumers to find what they're looking for by organising content in a way that makes sense.
Sitemaps and content hierarchies can be useful for this purpose.

Useful examples of user interface and navigation

1. A Search on Google:

One of the best examples of an intuitive user interface is Google's search page. It specialises in making it easy to get about, with results that are both relevant and well-organized.

Apple's iOS, version 2:

Apple's mobile OS has a reputation for its user-friendly design and navigation due to its consistent iconography and gesture-based navigation.

Spotify (No. 3):

Spotify's intuitive interface makes it simple to search for, sort, and play music.
- The experience is much improved by the clean tabs and simple search bar.

Four. Airbnb:
Airbnb's mobile app and desktop site both have polished interfaces and are easy to use.
- The user experience for finding lodging, narrowing down options, and reserving a property meets the highest standards.

Dropbox, number 5.

The Dropbox interface was designed with the user's ease of use and convenience in mind.
Folders, files, and sharing options can all be accessed directly from the menu.

Conclusion

Constantly learning more about your users and what they want can help you improve your design and navigation. Use these guidelines to make a digital product that not only draws in customers but also keeps them coming back for more. User engagement, conversion rates, and the overall success of your digital project are all directly impacted by the quality of the user interface and the ease of navigation it provides. If you want to succeed in today's rapidly evolving and fiercely competitive digital market, you must put the user experience front and centre, solicit feedback, and iterate on your design frequently.

Chapter 7:
Security and Settlements

7.1- Online payment options and gateways.

The foundation of e-commerce and digital exchanges is the availability of secure online payment methods and gateways. It is essential for companies of all sizes to be able to accept payments online in a safe and hassle-free manner. In this detailed manual, we'll talk about the several ways clients can pay you online, the payment gateways they can use, and the best practises for implementing them all together.

The Importance of Electronic Payments

The proliferation of online shopping and other forms of digital commerce has increased the importance of accepting payments online. Why do they matter?

1. Convenience: Customers have the choice to shop online whenever and wherever they like, thanks to the availability of several payment methods.

To further increase their consumer base, businesses can accept payments from people all around the world through online payment processors.

There is a direct correlation between the availability of several payment methods and an increase in sales, as customers are more likely to complete purchases that they have started.

Customers feel safe giving their financial information through payment gateways because it is encrypted during transmission.

5. Efficiency: Online payments expedite the transaction process, lowering administrative costs and eliminating the need for manual handling of payments.

Varieties of Available Online Payment Methods

Online merchants can accept a wide variety of payments from customers, depending on their preferences and the nature of the transaction.

Card Payments (Credit and Debit) 1.

   Credit and debit card payments processed by card networks like Visa, MasterCard, and American Express dominate the online payment market.
   - In order to accept credit card payments, either directly or through a payment gateway, businesses require a merchant account.

Second, Electronic Wallets:
   PayPal, Apple Pay, Google Pay, and Samsung Pay are just a few examples of digital wallets that make it possible to safely store payment information and make instant online purchases.
   They provide a simple, mouse-click purchasing option.

Money Transfers to the Bank

   Customers have the option of making payments straight from their bank accounts through bank transfers, such as ACH transfers or wire transactions.

Cryptocurrency is the fourth.

   Bitcoin, Ethereum, and Litecoin are just a few of the cryptocurrencies that are accepted as payment by some stores.

Payments made with cryptocurrencies are anonymous and decentralised.

Electronic checks:

E-checks, often known as electronic checks, are a digital replacement for paper checks. They are frequently used for subscriptions, recurrent payments, and business-to-business dealings.

Card prepayments:
Gift cards and prepaid debit cards give its owners access to a set amount of money that can be spent on goods and services. They find widespread use as presents and monetary resources.

Payment in Full (COD): 7.

Cash on delivery (COD) transactions involve the collection of payment in the form of cash upon delivery of the product to the consumer.
It's widely used in places where online payment methods are still in their infancy.

Payment Processors

To ensure the safety of financial information during online transactions, payment gateways operate as a middleman between customers, retailers, and banks. Many people use the following payment processors:

Stripe 1.

Stripe is a popular online payment processing service due to its excellent support for a wide variety of payment types and channels.

It has advanced features for preventing fraud and creating personalised checkout processes.

PayPal, number two:

PayPal is a well-known online payment system that allows users to send and receive money using their bank account, a credit or debit card, or their PayPal balance.

The payment procedure is simplified with PayPal's Express Checkout.

Square (3):

Square's online and in-person payment options make it a great choice for small businesses.

Various POS systems (hardware and software) are made available by this company.

Authorize.Net, number four:

Authorize.Net is a trusted payment gateway that has been around for a long time and accepts a variety of payment types. It can screen for fraudulent activity, bill users regularly, and accept electronic checks.

Braintree, number five:

Braintree is a PayPal subsidiary that facilitates online and mobile payments. It's secure, flexible, and works with a number of different payment ways.

6. Adyen:

Adyen has a large customer base around the world and accepts a variety of currencies and payment methods.

It's a one-stop shop for making purchases anywhere, anytime, on any device.

Guidelines for Establishing Secure Online Payments

Follow these guidelines for a safe and secure online payment experience:

First, Safeguards:

   Encryption (SSL/TLS) should be used to safeguard financial information while in transit.
   Adhere to the guidelines set forth by the PCI DSS (Payment Card Industry Data Security Standard).
   - Keep your payment processing software up-to-date and patched.

Second, Trust and Openness:

   Payment terms, fees, and return policies should all be made clear to clients.
   Exhibit security and trust badges to reassure customers.
Thirdly, "Responsive Design":
   Make sure that your payment pages are accessible on a variety of mobile devices.

Checkout, Step 4:

   Allow clients to make purchases as "guests" rather than requiring them to register for an account.

5. Handling Errors:

   If a financial transaction fails, make sure there are helpful error messages to read.
   Provide a way for customers to get in touch with help desk staff.

Testing, number six:

- Find and fix any usability problems with your payment system by conducting extensive testing.
- Make sure everything is still working by testing it regularly.

7. Optimising the User Experience:

Make the purchasing procedure as easy and quick as possible.
Reduce the number of clicks and fields on the order form to maximise conversions.

8. Updates Frequently:

Upgrade your secure online payment gateways and software when new features and fixes become available.

Adherence 9.

Keep up with the ever-evolving compliance and regulatory standards in your field and area.

Conclusion

These days, a business can't function without the ability to accept payments online. In order to satisfy their customers' varying tastes and keep their financial transactions safe and efficient, businesses need to accept a wide range of payment types. In order to build confidence, increase conversions, and sustain expansion in the digital marketplace, firms should apply best practises, use reputable payment gateways, and maintain a high level of security awareness.

7.2- Ensuring e-commerce security for customers.

When it comes to purchasing goods and services, the accessibility and variety offered by online marketplaces are unrivalled. But as the e-commerce market expands, so do the threats that come with making purchases online. Customers' confidence and private data must be protected when conducting business online. For the sake of everyone involved in the e-commerce process, this book will delve deeply into the strategies, best practises, and technology that can strengthen the safety of online transactions.

The Value of Safe Online Shopping

There are many important reasons why e-commerce security is essential:

Customers are more likely to feel comfortable making purchases and coming back for more if they know their information is safe in an online store.

To avoid fraud and identity theft, it is important to protect sensitive client data like payment and personal details.

Third, Legal Compliance: To avoid legal ramifications and fines, e-commerce enterprises must follow data protection laws and regulations.
4. Reputation Preservation: Customers may leave after hearing bad things about a company due to a security breach.

5. Business Continuity: Preventing security breaches keeps businesses running and brings in money as usual.

The Most Frequent Dangers to Online Stores

The first step in protecting yourself from danger is realising what you're up against. Examples of typical online shopping security risks include:

One sort of cyberattack is known as "phishing," and it involves the use of bogus websites or emails to deceive victims into giving over sensitive information.

Unauthorised access to client data, such as credit card information, can result in financial losses and legal implications.

Thirdly, Payment Card Fraud occurs when cybercriminals make fraudulent purchases using stolen card information.

Fourth, malicious software (often known as "malware") can infiltrate e-commerce websites or users' devices, allowing hackers to steal information or compromise security.
5: Distributed Denial of Service (DDoS) Attacks: Attackers flood a website with traffic to render it inaccessible or steal private information.

Hackers use Man-in-the-Middle Attacks to steal information or change transactions by intercepting communications between customers and websites.

Strategies and Recommended Procedures for Protecting Online Transactions

SSL (Secure Sockets Layer) Encryption Must Be Used First.

   SSL certificates will encrypt information sent between your website and your consumers' browsers.
   A valid SSL certificate that protects all necessary pages must be maintained.

Use Robust Authentication (2):

Customers' accounts should have robust, one-of-a-kind passwords. Add an extra safeguard by using MFA (multi-factor authentication).

Third, Update Software on a Regular Basis:
Update your e-commerce platform, add-ons, and other third-party solutions as soon as security updates become available.
Deprecated software can be a security risk, so it should be updated or removed.

4 Safe and Secure Transactions:

Put your trust in established payment gateways that follow the PCI DSS requirements.
Credit card numbers and other private payment details should never be saved on your server.

Regular audits and tests of security:

Keep an eye out for security flaws by scheduling routine audits.
To determine how secure your website is, conduct a penetration test.

Install a WAF to protect your web apps:

Common web assaults, such as SQL injection and XSS, can be warded off with the aid of a WAF.

7. Teaching the Customer:
- Teach your clientele how to spot phishing scams and maintain up-to-date software on their devices.

8. At-Rest Data Encryption:

Protect sensitive client information on your servers by encrypting it.

Management of Assets and Inventory

Keep track of all your digital assets and make sure your permissions and security settings are up to date.

Plan for Dealing with Emergencies Ten.

Create an efficient incident response plan to deal with security breaches immediately.
- Maintain open lines of communication with affected customers while adhering to all applicable rules.

Training in Security Awareness Eleven:

Educate your staff on cybersecurity best practises and the value of protecting sensitive client information.
Regulations Compliance (12):

- Learn about data protection laws that may apply to your company, such as the General Data Protection Regulation (GDPR) and the Health Insurance Portability and Accountability Act (HIPAA).

E-commerce Security Technologies and Tools

Firewalls, 1.

To prevent web application threats, Web Application Firewalls (WAFs) filter and monitor incoming traffic.

Security Add-ons:

Use security plugins that provide further defence against threats and vulnerabilities, if they are available for your e-commerce platform.

Thirdly, Encryption Software:

Use encryption software to safeguard information at rest and in transit. OpenSSL and Let's Encrypt are two popular alternatives for generating SSL certificates.

Security incident and event management (SIEM) is the fourth category.
SIEM solutions gather security data from a wide variety of sources and analyse it to help detect and deal with security events.

Virus and malware protection:
Antivirus and anti-malware software should be installed on your servers to ward off any attacks.
CDNs, or content distribution networks:
Using a content delivery network (CDN) can improve site performance and security by spreading traffic over different servers.

Scanners for Internet Safety (7):
Scan your e-commerce platform with automated technologies to find its weak spots.

Conclusion
Maintaining trust in online transactions calls for constant vigilance and innovation. Putting customer data protection first not only safeguards your company from financial and legal consequences, but also builds trust with your clientele. E-commerce security can be improved, common dangers can be mitigated, and a secure environment for online shoppers can be provided by following the advice in this article. Keep in mind that the duty of keeping private data safe falls on the shoulders of both the company and its clients.

7.3- Fraud prevention measures.

Businesses of all sizes and in all sectors of the economy are vulnerable to the widespread and expensive fraud that exists in today's digital world. Strong fraud prevention procedures are crucial for shielding your company and its consumers from fraud's potentially disastrous impacts. In this all-encompassing manual, we will delve into techniques, standards, and tools for thwarting fraud and protecting business operations.

Recognising the Importance of Taking Preventative Measures Against Fraud

There are many reasons why preventing fraud is essential to running a successful business:

(1) Financial Impact: Payment card fraud, identity theft, and other forms of fraud can all lead to significant financial losses for consumers and companies alike.

Second, fraud can have a negative impact on a company's reputation, which can discourage customers from interacting with the organisation in the future.

Thirdly, fraud can cause a disruption in routine business activities, which can lead to wasted time and money.

Legal and Regulatory Consequences 4. Businesses must adhere to data protection and fraud prevention standards. Penalties and obligations may be incurred if this is not done.

Fifthly, you'll gain your clients' trust by showing them that you take fraud protection seriously, which will make them feel more comfortable sharing their information with you.

Common Fraud Schemes

Many different kinds of fraudulent behaviour exist, but some of the most common are:

1. Payment Card Fraud: Criminals make purchases with stolen credit card information.

Second, fraudsters steal identification details with the purpose of using the victim's identity to commit financial crimes.

The third form of cybercrime is called "phishing," and it involves the use of fraudulent emails or websites to deceive victims into giving over personal information.

Fourthly, Account Takeover occurs when hackers obtain access to user accounts without permission.
5. Chargeback fraud occurs when a customer makes a false claim that they did not receive the goods or services they paid for.

Sixth, Friendly Fraud occurs when consumers initiate chargebacks by disputing lawful purchases on the grounds that they were not made by the consumer.

Best Practises and Anti-Fraud Strategies

Authentication of Users (1):

   Put in place rigorous user authentication procedures like CAPTCHA and multi-factor authentication (MFA).
   Insist that users make use of complex, memorable passwords that they update on a frequent basis.

To better Know Your Customer (KYC):

Collecting information from government-issued IDs or utility bills can help you confirm a customer's identification.
   - Make sure all high-risk financial dealings follow KYC procedures.

Identifying and tracking fraud:
   Use analytics powered by artificial intelligence to spot out-of-the-ordinary behaviour.
   Keep an eye out for suspicious activity in real time.

Fourth, Transaction Authentication:

   Make sure all your financial dealings are authentic by using a verification service like AVS or the CVV number on the back of your card.

AI and machine learning, number five:

   Use artificial intelligence and machine learning to spot red flags that could indicate fraud.

IP location tracking and device fingerprinting:

   Assess the veracity of user locations and devices by using IP geolocation and device fingerprinting.

7. Schooling and Instruction:

   - Teach workers how to spot fraudulent activity and educate them on the dangers of fraud.
   - Make security awareness a company-wide priority.
Safe and Sound Payment Methods, No. 8:
   Pick dependable payment processors who use state-of-the-art security and adhere to PCI DSS (Payment Card Industry Data Security Standard) requirements.

Data Encryption, Number Nine:

Protect sensitive client information with military-grade encryption at all times, not only while in transit.

Audits and scans for security flaws should be performed routinely.

To find and fix security holes in your systems, you should do frequent security audits and vulnerability assessments.

11. Analysis and Review of Transactions:

Identify possible instances of fraud by doing a manual evaluation of high-value or high-risk transactions.

12. Reporting and Customer Feedback:

- Urge your clientele to report any suspicious behaviour right away.
Improve safeguards against fraud by listening to and responding to patron comments.
Chargeback Administration:

Create efficient systems for managing chargebacks in order to resolve disputes quickly and cut down on losses.

Anti-Fraud Tools and Technology

1 Detection software for fraud:

Take use of specialised fraud detection software that scans for suspicious activity based on machine learning algorithms.

Services for Confirming Individuals' Identities

Use an outside service that verifies a user's identification to make sure they are who they say they are.

Services for IP-based Geolocation:

Utilise IP geolocation services to ascertain user locations and flag any out-of-the-ordinary behaviour.

Technology Identification Methods:

To analyse device characteristics and spot outliers, device fingerprinting technologies should be implemented.

Lastly, SIEM (Security Information and Event Management) Systems:

Utilise a security information and event management system to aggregate security event logs and spot outliers throughout your network.

Artificial Intelligence-Powered Fraud-Prevention Systems:

Think of unified platforms that can analyse financial transactions, consumer patterns, and other data for signs of fraud using AI.

Conclusion

To prevent fraud in the face of increasingly clever cybercriminals, firms must constantly adapt to new threats. Strengthen your fraud prevention efforts, protect your business and consumer data, and keep your customers' trust by using the strategies, best practises, and technologies detailed in this guide. In today's increasingly digital environment, it's crucial for businesses to take precautions against fraud to ensure their long-term survival and profitability.

Chapter 8:
Controlling Stock and Meeting Orders

8.1- Efficient inventory management techniques.

Businesses of all sizes and in all fields can benefit greatly from careful inventory management. It has a direct effect on profits by making sure the proper supplies are on hand when needed and reducing storage fees. The goal of this guide is to assist you achieve efficient inventory management so that you can streamline processes, cut expenses, and improve customer satisfaction.

Managing stock effectively is crucial.

There are a number of significant upsides to effective inventory management:

Reducing costs by minimising storage, insurance, and depreciation is the primary benefit of stock optimisation.

Second, Improved funds Flow: Effective management prevents resources from being squandered on surplus stock, which frees up funds for other uses.
Keeping enough inventory on hand increases consumer satisfaction and loyalty by making products readily available when they are needed.
There will be fewer instances of stockouts (when supplies run out) and overstock (when there is too much inventory) if supply and demand are both met.

5. Waste Reduction: Keeping outmoded or quickly expiring stock to a minimum helps cut costs and waste.

Methods and Recommendations for Effective Inventory Management

First, a [ABC Analysis]:

   Divide your stock into three groups, labelled A, B, and C, according to its relative importance and worth.
   High-value "A" goods are the most important for your company, so managing them should be a top priority.

Just-in-Time (JIT) Stockpiling:

   - Use Just-In-Time (JIT) inventory management to order and store items just in time. This not only keeps things fresh but also saves storage costs.

Thirdly, Security Stock:
   Determine safety stock volumes based on historical data and demand variability; keep safety stock levels at an appropriate level to absorb demand swings and supply chain disruptions.
4. EOQ (Economic Order Quantity):

   If you want to minimise your stock holding expenses, you should find the EOQ and order that much of a given item.
   Think about things like the price of ordering and maintaining inventory and how consistent the demand is.

VMI (Vendor Managed Inventory) 5.

   Work together with your vendors and provide them access to real-time data to manage your stock.
   VMI helps you have appropriate stock on hand at a reduced holding cost.

Demand Prediction, Number Six:

   Demand may be precisely predicted with the help of past sales information, market trends, and comments from satisfied customers.

Improve the precision of your predictions by using state-of-the-art techniques and computational tools.

7. FIFO and LIFO:

Inventory costing strategies such as FIFO and LIFO should be used to efficiently handle time-sensitive or easily spoiled goods.

8. Frequent Inspections and Counts:

Maintain accurate records by doing cycle counts and conducting regular physical audits of inventories.

9. Partnerships with Suppliers:

Improve delivery times, save costs, and secure early access to sales by building and maintaining excellent connections with your suppliers.

Technology and automation, number ten:

Spend money on automation software and hardware to keep tabs on stock levels in real time.
To keep tabs on everything precisely, implement barcodes and RFID technologies.

11. Tracking of Batches and Lots:

In the event of a recall or quality issue, it is important to be able to track individual batches or lots of items.

ABC/XYZ Dissection:
Classify stock according to value and demand variability using a combination of ABC and XYZ analysis. This is useful for determining which methods of stock management to employ for which product types.

Packages in Large Quantities:

If you're looking to save money on shipping, but don't want to run out of space, consider placing a large order.

14 Decreased Lead Times:

Reduce product delivery times by working with suppliers to cut down on extra waiting time.

15 Interdepartmental Teamwork:

Encourage teamwork across functions like sales, marketing, and operations to reach consensus on inventory management objectives.

Technology and methods for managing stockpiles

First, Supply Chain Management:
Make use of specialised software for managing stock that allows for real-time monitoring, demand forecasting, and reporting.
Secondly, RFID and Barcode Systems:

Barcode and RFID technology can help automate inventory management and cut down on human error.

Thirdly, ERP Systems (Enterprise Resource Planning):

The inventory management modules included in ERP systems help to synchronise stock levels with other operational metrics.

Software for predicting future demand

- Invest in technologies that can accurately predict future demand using sophisticated algorithms and data analytics.

Fifthly, Point of Sale (POS) Systems:

Better inventory management and planning can be achieved with the use of point-of-sale (POS) systems that record sales in real time.

Managing a warehouse with a WMS.

Warehouse management systems help streamline processes including stock receiving, picking, packaging, and shipping.

Conclusion

It takes constant attention and optimisation of many moving parts to achieve effective inventory management. A well-balanced inventory that satisfies consumer demand, lowers costs, and improves operational efficiency can be achieved by following the strategies and recommendations presented in this manual. The objective is to find a happy medium between keeping enough stock on hand to meet consumer demands and minimising holding costs to maximise profits. Your company may thrive in today's dynamic business environment by employing effective inventory management tactics and solutions.

8.2- Different fulfillment options (e.g., dropshipping, warehousing).

When running a firm that deals in tangible goods, fulfilment is essential. Distributing goods to consumers in a timely and effective manner. Decisions about how orders are fulfilled can have a significant effect on customer happiness, productivity, and the bottom line. This tutorial will walk you through the ins and outs of various fulfilment strategies, such as dropshipping, warehousing, and hybrid approaches, so that you can make the best choice for your company.

The Basics of E-Commerce Fulfilment

Orders placed through an online store go through several stages of fulfilment before being delivered to the customer. These measures may change based on the selected method of delivery. Important aspects of happiness include:

Accepting, checking, and fulfilling orders placed by customers is the first step in Order Processing.

2. Inventory Management: Controlling supply and demand to never run out of a product.

Thirdly, Picking and Packing entails obtaining ordered items from stock, packing them safely, and creating shipping labels.
shipment is the process of assigning a delivery date, picking a shipment method and company, and sending out the package.

5. Delivery: Making sure the product is delivered to the customer on time.

Alternatives for Providing Service

The Dropshipping Method

A retailer who uses dropshipping to satisfy orders does not retain inventory on hand. Instead, retailers like Amazon buy products from third parties (often wholesalers or manufacturers) and have them shipped straight to customers.

Advantages: - You won't have to spend money on stockpiling or storing.
Reduced outlay of capital.
The ability to scale and adapt.

The downside is that you have less say over the final product's quality and availability.
Lower profit margins as a result of wholesalers' reduced margins.
- Third-party suppliers could cause shipping delays or other problems.
Second, In-House Storage :

When a store uses in-house storage, products are kept in a facility that either belongs to the store or is leased by the store. When a consumer places an order, the store fulfils it by selecting, packing, and shipping the item.

Full management of stock, quality, and order fulfilment are all advantages.
Improved shipment speed and dependability.
Possible financial benefits from making larger purchases and making better use of available space.

Higher initial expenditures for storage space, personnel, and inventory.
Constant upkeep and safety-related costs.
In the event of demand fluctuations, there is little room for manoeuvre.

3rd Party Logistics (3PL):

Third-party logistics providers (3PLs) are businesses that facilitate the storage and distribution of goods. Third-party logistics providers (3PLs) store goods for retailers and process, select, pack, and ship orders.

Advantages: Having access to specialised logistical knowledge.
- The capacity to expand without spending more on new facilities.
Possible financial gains from pooling assets.

Cons: - Giving up some say in the fulfilment process.
- Expenses for third-party logistics providers.
- Difficulties in effective communication if your company and the 3PL's are not in close alignment.

Hybrid Accomplishment, 4.

- Functioning In Detail: Hybrid fulfilment integrates features of many fulfilment models. A store may use dropshipping for some products while relying on in-house or 3PL warehousing for others.

The ability to shift gears and accommodate fluctuating supply and demand is a definite plus.
- Increased product-specific cost effectiveness through individualised strategy development.
- Greater agency over vital determinants of happiness.

Cons: Downsides - Managing and coordinating multiple fulfilment methods can be complicated.
Potentially more difficult to keep track of and report on.
Potential for increased operational costs if properly managed.

Choosing the Best Distribution Method

There are a number of elements to consider when deciding which fulfilment strategy is best for your organisation.

1 - Product Type: Think about the size, fragility, and unique handling/storage needs of your products.

Second, have a look at how many orders your company is getting. Dropshipping may be more practical for smaller firms than in-house or 3PL warehousing for larger ones.

Third, consider your system's ability to expand. Think about how well your preferred fulfilment method handles changes in demand.

Control Step four: decide how much say you want to have in stock keeping, product quality, and the rest of the fulfilment process.

5. Costs: Examine the monetary factors, including the initial investment, the monthly maintenance, and the possible savings.

Sixth, Shipping Speed: Think about how long it takes to ship products to clients and whether or not your fulfilment strategy can keep up with their expectations.
Considering international shipping and customs regulations is an important consideration if your target market covers numerous regions or nations, which brings us to our seventh point: Geographic Reach.

Issues and Things to Think About

It's important to keep in mind the following things regardless of which fulfilment method is selected:

1. Inventory Management: Precise recording of stock levels is essential to averting stockouts and surpluses.

2. Quality Control: Always use rigorous procedures for checking that things are in perfect condition before shipping them to clients.

Third, utilise Technology and Integration by integrating powerful inventory management tools and systems with your web store.

4. Returns Handling: Set up a transparent and streamlined procedure for processing returns and exchanging items.

5. Shipping: Select trustworthy shipping partners and refine shipping techniques to cut down on expenses while maximising productivity.

Conclusion

Customer satisfaction, operational efficiency, and profitability are all directly influenced by how well an online store handles fulfilment. It's important to consider the specifics of your business and its fulfilment needs before deciding between dropshipping, in-house warehousing, third-party warehousing, and hybrid fulfilment. You can select the fulfilment option that best fits your business plan and puts you on the way to providing excellent client experiences by carefully considering your items, order volume, scalability, control preferences, and prices. Keep in mind that fulfilment is not a fixed process but rather one that can vary as your company does.

8.3- Order processing and shipping logistics.

Successful online stores rely heavily on streamlined order management and shipping procedures. These procedures guarantee timely and accurate shipment of customer orders. Best practises, technological options, and methods to optimise your operations and increase customer happiness are just some of the topics covered in this all-encompassing guide on order processing and shipping logistics.

Logistics in taking orders and delivering packages:

Several factors make order processing and shipment logistics essential to the e-commerce ecosystem:

Customers are more likely to return as a result of a great experience and to recommend your business to others if their orders are processed quickly and correctly.

Order fulfilment and logistics that are well-oiled machines save money, cut down on mistakes, and make the most of available assets; this is what we mean by "Operational Efficiency."

Thirdly, inventory management relies on accurate order processing to keep stock at just the right quantity to avoid both shortages and surpluses.

Competitive Advantage 4 Streamlined operations allow organisations to offer competitive shipping choices, such as quick delivery and cost-effective shipping rates.

Data insights number five: the information gleaned from customers' order histories can shed light on their habits and preferences, allowing for more calculated business moves.

Important Order Processing Components

In the e-commerce supply chain, order processing entails a number of crucial procedures, including the following:

First, you'll need to perform an order verification to ensure all of your customers' orders have been processed correctly.

Checking stock levels in real time is a great way to make sure products are still available for purchase.

Thirdly, Payment Processing entails safely processing payments while confirming the validity of the payment mechanism and the legitimacy of the transaction.

Fourth, "Picking and Packing" involves retrieving the ordered goods from stock, placing them in protective packaging, and printing out shipping labels.
Package size, weight, final location, and expected delivery time all play a role in determining the best shipping method and carrier to use. 5.

Create shipping labels and supporting paperwork, such as tracking numbers, for outgoing packages.

Send clients shipment confirmations and tracking numbers so they know where their orders are at all times.

8. Quality Control: Perform quality inspections to make sure things are up to par before they are shipped.

9. Returns Processing: Clearly define how returns and exchanges are processed to maximise efficiency.

Recommended Methods for Speeding Up the Ordering Process

First, Automation: Eliminate human data entry and processing errors by automating order processing. Purchase an OMS or integrated e-commerce platform to streamline your business's order processing.

Second, implement a system for keeping track of stock levels in real time to avoid overselling and shortages.

Third, you should optimise your shipping rates by using shipping rate calculators and negotiating lower delivery costs with carriers.

4. Multi-Channel Integration: Integrate with a central system to streamline order processing across multiple sales channels (e.g., website, marketplace, brick-and-mortar).

5. Batch Processing: Collectively processing orders in bulk to cut down on time spent on processing each order individually.

6. Customer Communication: Ensure that customers are updated on the status of their orders from the time they are placed until they are delivered.

Quality Control: Conduct pre-shipment inspections to guarantee all products are up to par before they are sent out.

Important Parts of Logistics Shipping

Logistics in shipping pertain to the preparation, carrying out, and controlling of shipments. Important features include:

1. Carrier Selection: Select carriers based on package dimensions, weight, final location, and expected arrival time.

mailing Labels: Create labels that provide the correct mailing address and tracking number for each package.

Third, Package Packaging: Preserve goods as little as possible throughout shipping by using suitable packaging materials.

Freight management include coordinating and negotiating freight rates for larger shipments.

Fifth, live shipment tracking so that customers may see how their orders are coming along.

Prepare and submit all customs papers for foreign shipments to ensure a speedy and easy border crossing.

7. Delivery Confirmation: Obtain confirmation of delivery, signatures, or images of delivered items to confirm delivery.

Logistical Best Practises

Obtain reasonable shipping costs from carriers by discussing your shipping volume and needs with them.

Second, Shipping software: Invest in shipping software that interfaces with your e-commerce platform to simplify label generation and order tracking.

Third, implement a multi-carrier strategy to provide clients with a variety of delivery options, including express, standard, and economy.
Reduce dimensional weight charges and maximise product security without sacrificing package efficiency.
Fifthly, set up effective Reverse Logistics procedures for dealing with consumer returns, exchanges, and questions.

Having an understanding of international shipping regulations, customs processes, and duties is essential if you plan on sending internationally.

Use route optimisation tools to shorten delivery times and lower transportation expenses.

Shipping Industry Technology Answers

Consider implementing the following technological solutions to improve shipping operations and order processing:

1. Order Management System (OMS): An OMS consolidates order handling by automating processes and connecting with a number of different channels for taking payments and delivering packages.

Shipping software streamlines the process of creating shipping labels, comparing rates, and keeping tabs on orders. ShipStation, Shippo, and Easyship are three of the most well-known choices.

Overselling and stockouts can be avoided with the help of an inventory management system, which is made possible by the use of inventory management software.

In order to streamline your business processes, you should connect your e-commerce platform (such Shopify, WooCommerce, or Magento) with your shipping and order management tools.

Conclusion

The success of your online store depends on your ability to efficiently manage orders and shipment. By following best practices, using digital solutions, and maintaining a focus on customer satisfaction, you can optimize these essential parts of your supply chain. The development and profitability of an e-commerce business depend on the quality of the client experience they provide, and this may be improved by streamlining order processing and shipping.

Chapter 9:
Decision Making Through Analysing Data

9.1- Gathering and analyzing e-commerce data.

Data is a valuable resource in the ever-changing landscape of e-commerce, as it can facilitate well-informed decision making, improve customer experiences, and fuel expansion. To maintain a competitive edge and realise sustained success in the online marketplace, it is essential to collect and analyse data from online transactions. In this all-inclusive manual, we'll delve into the value of e-commerce data, the ideal methods for gathering it, and the techniques for drawing meaningful conclusions from it.

The Importance of Online Shopping Statistics

The term "e-commerce data" is used to describe the vast amount of information gathered from online stores, communications with customers, and user actions. For a variety of reasons, this information is priceless:

1. Customer Insights: E-commerce data provides a thorough understanding of customer behaviour, preferences, and purchasing habits, allowing firms to personalise their goods and marketing campaigns.
Performance Metrics 2: Information helps evaluate the success of things like advertising campaigns, product launches, and the functionality of websites so that changes may be made based on the collected information.

3. Inventory Management: Avoiding stockouts, overstocks, and waste requires accurate data on product demand and inventory levels.

Fourth, Competitive Intelligence can be gained by analysing e-commerce data in order to keep tabs on the competition, spot emerging market trends, and seize profitable business possibilities.

Data-driven personalization improves the consumer experience through the provision of individualised information, product suggestions, and discounts. 5. Personalization.

6. Fraud Detection: Businesses and customers are both safeguarded by data analysis's ability to detect and stop fraudulent transactions.

Recommended Methods for Collecting Data

Meaningful analysis relies on accurate data collection. The following are guidelines for effective data collection:

Key metrics must be defined first. Figure out which pieces of information and KPIs are most important for achieving your business objectives. Some examples of such metrics are conversion rates, the cost of acquiring a new customer, and shopping cart abandonment. Data sources can include your website, mobile apps, social networking platforms, and third-party analytics tools, so it's important to identify all of them.

(3) Data Tracking: Utilise reliable tracking techniques, such as Google Analytics or bespoke tracking scripts, to reliably gather key data points.

Fourth, Data Accuracy: Audit and validate data frequently to maintain precision. Resolve any inconsistencies immediately.

5. consumer Consent: Obtain consumer permission to collect data as required by data privacy legislation (e.g., GDPR, CCPA).

6. Data Storage: Keep information in a safe place, using sound data protection practises.

7. Data Integration: Consolidate data from multiple sources into one easily accessible location for analysis.

Whenever feasible, collect and analyse data in real-time so that you may act on it as it happens.

Data governance refers to the processes and policies put in place to guarantee high data standards are consistently met.

Strategies for Efficient Analysis of Online Shopping Data

The next phase, after data collection, is to analyse it for insights. Tips for Efficient Data Analysis in Electronic Commerce

1. Segmentation: Classify your clientele into subsets according to demographics, buying habits, and other criteria. Insights specific to each subsection can be gleaned through individual analysis.

A/B Testing: Run A/B testing to see which product descriptions, prices, or website layouts perform better to see which ones are more appealing to buyers.

Sales Funnel Analysis is a method for monitoring and analysing the steps a customer takes from first contact to final purchase. The areas of greatest client attrition can then be targeted for improvement.

To uncover trends and retention patterns, Cohort Analysis groups consumers who made their initial purchase during the same time frame (a cohort) and examines their behaviour over time.

5. Predictive Analytics: Make use of predictive analytics to look ahead and make proactive decisions about sales, consumer behaviour, and market trends.

6. client Lifetime Value (CLV): Determine the value of a client over time and set priorities for customer retention based on this number.

To better educate your cross-selling and up-selling efforts, consider conducting a "basket analysis" of the things your consumers typically buy together.

8. Market Basket Analysis: Analyse the most common items bought together by shoppers to fine-tune your product suggestions and sales pitches.

Monitor social media channels and analyse brand sentiment to determine client satisfaction and find opportunities for growth.

Competitive Analysis 10: Learn how to outperform the competition by analysing their pricing methods, product lines, and consumer feedback.

Reporting and Data Visualisation

Insights and trends can be efficiently communicated through data visualisation. Data visualisation and reporting can benefit from the following methods:

1. Dashboards: Display real-time data and key performance indicators with individualised dashboards built with tools like Tableau, Power BI, or Google Data Studio.

Utilise visual representations like bar charts, line graphs, and heatmaps to simplify the display of complex data.

Thirdly, heatmaps can assist you optimise the design and layout of your website by revealing trends in how users interact with it.

Funnel Visualisations, number four, show the steps of the client journey and point out weak spots.

5. Geospatial Maps: Display the location of your customers, sales, or other important data on a map.

Security and Confidentiality of Data

Keeping customers' personal information safe is of utmost importance in the online shopping world. Protect client information by encrypting sensitive data and putting in place stringent security measures, all while adhering to data privacy standards.

Conclusion

In today's digital business ecosystem, collecting and analysing e-commerce data is more than just a best practise; it's a strategic need. Businesses may improve customer experiences, expand their operations, and make better decisions with the help of data-driven insights. E-commerce companies can use data to their advantage by following best practises in data collection, investing in strong analysis strategies, and employing effective data visualisation techniques in order to maintain a competitive edge, respond quickly to shifting market conditions, and forge meaningful connections with loyal customers. Keep in mind that data analysis is a continuing procedure, the refining of which is crucial for keeping up with the rapidly developing e-commerce sector.

9.2- Using data to make informed business decisions.

In today's data-driven corporate market, the ability to use data to make strategic decisions is essential for long-term success. Data is used by companies across sectors, including e-commerce, to better comprehend consumer habits, enhance business processes, and plan for the future. The value of data, how to make good decisions based on data, and how data may revolutionise business tactics are all topics we'll cover in depth in this tutorial.

The Importance of Using Data to Make Choices

Using information gleaned from data, analytics, and insights to shape business decisions is what we call "data-driven decision-making." The importance of this method can't be emphasised enough:

Data gives accurate knowledge, minimising reliance on intuition and gut feeling, and thereby improving the quality of decisions made. Decisions are improved because of this.

2. Competitive Advantage: Businesses that properly exploit data get an advantage by spotting patterns, openings, and dangers in the marketplace.

3. Improved consumer Experiences: Insights gleaned from data allow companies to customise consumer interactions, offerings, and satisfaction.
Four, Resource Optimisation: Data aids in allocating resources efficiently, optimising operations and lowering expenses.

5. Risk Mitigation: By recognising risks and vulnerabilities through data analysis, firms can take preemptive action to lessen the likelihood of problems.

6. Innovation Catalyst: Information can provide fresh insights and possibilities for innovation, which in turn fuels business expansion and sets companies apart from their competitors.

Data-driven decision making best practises

The first step in making decisions based on data is to establish clear objectives. Your data approach might be better directed by knowing your end goals.

Second, watch out for your Data Quality by making sure everything is correct and up to date. Good decisions can't be made without accurate and trustworthy information.

3. Data Governance: Create policies and procedures for data governance in order to keep data quality, security, and compliance with applicable requirements at a high level of importance.
In order to have a full picture of how things are going for your company, it's a good idea to integrate data from a number of different places into one central database.
5. Advanced Analytics: Employ cutting-edge analytics methods like machine learning and predictive modelling to glean useful information from data.

To make the most of everyone's knowledge and experience, it's important to foster cross-functional collaboration throughout teams and departments.

7. Regular Data Audits: Conduct regular audits of your data to detect abnormalities, outliers, and other problems with data quality.

8. Data Visualisation: Represent complicated data in simple charts, graphs, and dashboards using data visualisation tools.

9. Real-Time Data: Use real-time data whenever feasible to make quick judgements and react to changing market conditions.

Ten. Ongoing Education: Provide opportunities for learning and growth to all staff members in order to boost data literacy and analytical prowess throughout the company.

The Disruptive Power of Data on Business Techniques

Customer-Centric Methods, No. 1: By analysing consumer data, firms can learn about their tastes, habits, and problems. This data is used to shape future products, advertising initiatives, and support policies with the end goal of giving customers a better experience.

2. Personalization: Based on a consumer's prior interactions and preferences, businesses can tailor content, product recommendations, and marketing messages to each unique customer.

3. Inventory Management: Overstocking and stockouts are avoided by data-driven demand forecasting and inventory optimisation, which also lowers carrying costs and boosts operational efficiency.

4. Effective Marketing: By focusing on the correct demographic with the right message at the right moment, businesses can increase their marketing budget's return on investment.

5. Supply Chain Optimisation: The enhanced insight afforded by data allows for the optimisation of sourcing, production, and distribution, which in turn reduces costs and shortens delivery times.

Risk management is the process through which a company prepares for and responds to potential threats, such as those posed by the stock market, cyberattacks, or regulatory oversight.

Competitive Analysis 7. Data analytics enables firms to keep tabs on the competition, follow market trends, and locate areas where they can fill in the gaps or seize new opportunities.

Issues and Things to Think About

While data-driven decision-making has many positive effects, it does not come without obstacles.

(1) Data Privacy: To safeguard customers' rights and stay out of court, businesses must carefully handle customers' personal information and adhere to data privacy legislation (e.g., GDPR, CCPA).

Second, make sure your data is encrypted and safe from hackers by using strict security protocols.

Thirdly, having access to an excessive amount of information might be confusing. Pay close attention to gathering and analysing information that supports your goals.

In order to make the transition to a data-driven culture, it may be necessary to make adjustments to the organization's structure, procedures, and way of thinking.

Allocating resources for data gathering, storage, and analysis can be expensive. 5. Analyse the return on investment of your data projects.

Conclusion

In today's highly competitive market, companies who understand how to leverage data to inform their decisions will succeed. Organisations may make better decisions, reach operational excellence, boost customer happiness, and stay ahead of the curve by adopting best practises in data collection, analysis, and governance and incorporating data-driven insights into their plans. Data is more than simply a resource; it's a strategic asset that can help firms adapt to the digital economy and achieve long-term success.

9.3- Key performance indicators (KPIs) for e-commerce success.

Understanding your company's performance is just as important as making sales in the fast-paced world of e-commerce. Your online business needs Key Performance Indicators (KPIs) as a rudder to steer you towards optimal performance. In this all-inclusive book, we'll delve into the most crucial key performance indicators (KPIs) for thriving online stores, their significance, and the best practises for utilising them to boost revenue and sales.

What Key Performance Indicators Mean for Online Stores

Key performance indicators are measurable measurements that reveal information about the well-being and success of your online store. They have a number of important advantages:

First, Key Performance Indicators (KPIs) enable data-driven decision making by providing a means of gauging the success of strategies and operations.

Key performance indicators (KPIs) aid in goal alignment by linking organisational targets to quantifiable outputs.

Third, by keeping an eye on key performance indicators, you can spot development openings, spots for enhancement, and problems in the making before they escalate.

4. Resource Allocation: Key performance indicators aid in resource allocation by directing time, energy, and money to the areas with the greatest potential for return.

Five, Competitive Analysis: Knowing where you stand in the market is as simple as comparing your key performance indicators (KPIs) to those of your competitors and the industry as a whole.

E-commerce key performance indicators

The percentage of site visitors that do the intended action (in this case, making a purchase) is referred to as the "conversion rate." Successful website design and advertising will result in a high conversion rate.

The percentage of shoppers who place an item in their basket but then abandon it before making a purchase is known as the "Cart Abandonment Rate." Keep an eye on this key performance indicator to find roadblocks to conversion.

Third, the Average Order Value (AOV) refers to the typical sum a consumer spends in a single order. Without adding new clients, revenue can be increased by increasing AOV.

4. Customer Acquisition Cost (CAC): The sum spent on promotional and marketing activities to bring in a new client. Profitability is increased by reducing CAC.
The amount of money you expect a customer to spend with your company over the course of their whole relationship with you is called their "customer lifetime value," or CLV for short. It's reasonable to put money into customer retention if their CLV is high.

The percentage of buyers that return for more is called the "Repeat Purchase Rate." A customer's lifetime value increases as they become a repeat buyer.

Churn rate, or the percentage of customers who cease buying from you, appears in position seven. Customer retention is directly proportional to the rate at which churn is reduced.

8. Traffic Sources: Examine the various channels (organic search, paid search, social media, and referrals) that send visitors to your website. You can use this in your advertising because of.

The percentage of people who click on a particular link (to a product or category, for example) is called the "click-through rate" (CTR). Click-through rate (CTR) is an essential metric for gauging the success of advertising and email marketing efforts.

The percentage of site visitors that only see a single page before leaving is known as the "bounce rate." There could be problems with the site's layout or content if the bounce rate is high.

11. Inventory Turnover Rate: The frequency with which stock is sold and replenished during a given time frame. A high inventory turnover rate is indicative of well-managed stock.

Gross profit margin (12) is the amount of money left over after expenses have been deducted from total sales. The health of a business can be gauged by keeping a close eye on the gross profit margin.

The Net Promoter Score (NPS) asks customers, "On a scale of 0-10, how likely are you to recommend our product/service to a friend or colleague?" to determine how satisfied and loyal they are.

Metrics like the percentage of emails opened, clicked on, and unsubscribed from can shed light on how successful your email marketing initiatives have been.

15. Response Time, or the typical amount of time it takes to address a customer's question or problem. When questions are answered quickly, customers are more satisfied.

16. Mobile Conversion Rate: The percentage of visitors who convert when using a mobile device. With more and more people making purchases on their phones, this indicator is crucial for making improvements to the mobile shopping experience.

Key Performance Indicators (KPIs)

The first step is to Define Clear Goals for each Key Performance Indicator. Direction and meaning can be found in one's goals.

Second, Regular Monitoring: Keep an eye on key performance indicators (KPIs) in real time or on a regular basis to spot changes.

Third, Benchmarking: Evaluate your key performance indicators (KPIs) in comparison to those of your competitors and the industry as a whole.

4. Segmentation: Examine Key Performance Indicators (KPIs) by client groups, product categories, or marketing channels to unearth insights that fuel specialised approaches.

5. A/B Testing: Use A/B tests to try out new ideas for your e-commerce operations and see how they affect key performance indicators.Sixth, "Data Integration: Integrate data from various sources, such as your e-commerce platform, CRM, and analytics tools, to get a holistic view of your business."Seventh, Feedback Loop: Let key performance indicator (KPI) data inform your approach. Make changes to your strategy in light of new information.

Conclusion

Key performance indicators are the map you use to navigate your online store. You can make better decisions, enhance productivity, and propel expansion by keeping an eye on and analysing these key variables. Keep in mind that your key performance indicators (KPIs) should reflect the aims of your organisation. In order to adjust quickly to shifts in the market and in consumer preferences, it is crucial to assess and modify your key performance indicators on a regular basis. In the end, your e-commerce company's long-term success and growth will depend on how well you use key performance indicators.

Chapter 10:
Online Shopping's Bright Future

10.1- Emerging trends in e-commerce (e.g., AI, VR).

Because of rapid technological development and shifting consumer tastes, e-commerce is a rapidly expanding sector. Maintaining a competitive edge in the e-commerce space calls for constant monitoring of the shifting winds that will determine the future of shopping online. Artificial Intelligence (AI), Virtual Reality (VR), and numerous others are poised to revolutionise the way we shop and sell online, and we will examine them in depth in this book.

One, Machine Learning and Artificial Intelligence (AI)

There are many ways in which AI is revolutionising online retail:

- Personalization: Artificial intelligence systems examine user information to tailor advertising, product listings, and other content to each individual.

- Chatbots and Virtual Assistants: Chatbots and virtual assistants powered by artificial intelligence (AI) respond to client questions in real time.
- Inventory Management: Businesses may save money and increase efficiency by avoiding wasteful overstocking and stockouts with the help of AI-driven demand forecasting and inventory optimisation. Machine learning algorithms predict client behaviour, allowing businesses to fine-tune their advertising and product-recommendation strategies with this information.

The use of photos in product searches has increased thanks to visual search made possible by AI.

Smart speakers and voice-activated shopping

Voice shopping is growing popularity as voice-activated smart speakers like Amazon's Alexa and Google Home become more widely available to consumers.

- Voice Shopping: Consumers may now place orders by voice commands, streamlining the shopping experience and introducing novel opportunities for the e-commerce industry.

- Voice Search Optimisation: Because voice search is different from text search, companies are adapting their content and offerings to accommodate it.

Smart speakers can be used as a shopper's personal shopper, assisting with product research, price comparisons, and order placement.

Third, Virtual Reality (VR) and Augmented Reality (AR)
The use of augmented and virtual reality is reshaping the shopping process:

Customers can digitally try on clothing, accessories, and cosmetics, cutting down on in-store try-ons and exchanges.

- Augmented Reality Product Visualisation: AR apps let consumers see how furniture, decor, and appliances would look in their own homes before making a purchase.

- Immersive Shopping Experiences: Virtual reality (VR) offers immersive shopping environments, giving users the feel of physically exploring a store and its contents.

(4) Blockchain and Cryptocurrency (4)

Blockchain technology improves the safety and openness of online financial dealings:

Blockchain's secure and tamper-resistant payment processing helps lower the potential for fraud.

- Transparency: Using blockchain-based tracking, consumers may confirm a product's genuineness and a seller's legitimacy.
To provide their customers more options, certain e-commerce sites may accept cryptocurrency payments.

Five. Social Business

Online markets are expanding into the realm of social media.

Shoppable posts can be made on social media platforms like Instagram and Facebook, allowing customers to buy things right from the post.

Sales and interest in a business can be boosted with the help of social media influencers who post positive reviews and recommendations of products.

Product presentations and sales can now take place in real time thanks to live streaming on social media sites, sometimes known as live shopping.

Sixthly: Ethical and Sustainable Online Shopping

Ethical and ecologically responsible online shopping is growing in popularity as people become more aware of their impact on the planet.

- Environmentally Friendly Products: Companies are making it a priority to provide environmentally friendly products, reduce packaging waste, and lessen their overall impact on the environment.

Businesses are open about their sourcing methods, and customers want to buy goods that were produced in an ethical manner.

To lessen their environmental impact, companies are looking into circular economy strategies like recycling and refurbishing.

7. E-Commerce Subscriptions

The popularity of subscription-based business models continues to spread across industries.

- Subscription Boxes: Companies curate and ship subscription boxes filled with unique goods, delighting customers with both familiar and unexpected items.

- Content Subscriptions: Streaming services, news websites, and online education platforms all provide paid memberships to their content libraries.

In addition to boosting client loyalty, subscription models generate consistent revenue for organisations.

8. Developments in Mobile Commerce (M-commerce)

Improvements in mobile commerce have resulted from the rise in smartphone usage:
- Progressive Web Apps (PWAs): PWAs provide a streamlined, hassle-free, and offline-capable mobile purchasing experience.

- Mobile Wallets: Mobile payment solutions like Apple Pay and Google Pay are rising in popularity because of the convenience they bring to the shopping process.

Businesses are increasingly placing an emphasis on designing their websites and apps with mobile users in mind.

9. Delivery using UAVs and other autonomous systems

For more rapid and cost-effective transport, drone and autonomous delivery systems are currently undergoing testing and implementation.

Drones and autonomous vehicles make next-day and same-day delivery possible at lower costs and in less time.

To reach clients in crowded urban regions, companies are looking into last-mile delivery options.

10 On-Demand Manufacturing and 3D Printing

The advent of 3D printing and just-in-time production has made it possible to cut inventory costs and increase individualization. Products like clothing, jewellery, and home decor can be customised by the buyer before they are made.

On-demand production minimises waste and storage fees by eliminating the need for stockpiles.

Privacy and Security of Personal Information

Data privacy and security are becoming important as data breaches grow more frequent.

- Data Protection Regulations: To protect consumer information, businesses must follow data protection regulations like GDPR and CCPA.

In order to keep sensitive client data safe, e-commerce companies employ stringent cybersecurity procedures.

Services for Managing Subscriptions

Companies are embracing subscription management tools to better manage invoicing, client retention, and churn as the demand for subscription services grows.

Conclusion

The e-commerce industry is dynamic because it responds to new technologies and shifting consumer preferences. In order to stay competitive and fulfil the changing expectations of customers, firms must adopt these new developments. E-commerce enterprises can better position themselves for long-term success in the ever-changing digital marketplace if they keep up with the latest developments, adopt new technologies, and constantly optimise their strategy.

10.2- The impact of changing consumer behaviors.

The online retail sector would cease to exist without consumers' actions. To be competitive, e-commerce enterprises must change as customers' tastes, behaviours, and expectations shift. In this all-encompassing book, we'll look at how shifting consumer habits have had a dramatic effect on the e-commerce industry, as well as the most effective ways to adapt to the current climate.

Digital Age Consumer Behaviour

Consumer behaviour towards companies has also changed with the advent of the digital age. As a result, some noteworthy changes in consumer behaviour have emerged:

One Online purchasing Preference: Customers increasingly favour purchasing online over visiting traditional stores due to the ease and selection available there.

With the proliferation of smartphones, mobile purchases are becoming the standard. Customers anticipate an uninterrupted mobile journey from discovery to purchase.

Thirdly, Personalization Expectations: Customers want more and more customised services based on their individual tastes.
The influence of social media on consumer behaviour is substantial. Influencer and peer recommendations have an impact on consumer behaviour.

Consumers today are very price-conscious; they utilise price-comparison websites and other price-tracking apps to locate the greatest prices.

6. Sustainability and Ethical Values: Many consumers place a premium on purchasing products that are created in a sustainable and ethical manner.

Subscription services have become increasingly commonplace in a variety of markets, from media streaming to home delivery of prepared meals.

There has been an increase in the demand for expedited shipping services such as next-day and same-day delivery.

Review and rating sites have a huge impact on customers' confidence and final purchases.

How Shifting Consumer Habits Affect Online Shopping

1. Improved Online Shopping: E-commerce companies are investing in customer-friendly website design, simple navigation, and mobile optimisation to meet shoppers' growing need for a streamlined online purchasing experience.

Data-driven personalization strategies like product recommendations and dynamic content are being utilised to provide shoppers with experiences that are unique to them.

Thirdly, Social Commerce: E-commerce companies are using social media for direct selling by incorporating "buy" buttons, shoppable postings, and influencer collaborations to tap into consumers' social influence.

4. Competitive Pricing Strategies: Businesses rely heavily on dynamic pricing algorithms, discounts, and loyalty programmes to woo price-conscious customers.

5. Sustainability Initiatives: In order to better reflect the values of their customers and lessen their negative influence on the environment, many online retailers are emphasising the importance of sustainable and ethical sourcing practises.

Subscription-based e-commerce businesses, which give consumers convenience and customised experiences, have seen rapid expansion in recent years.

E-commerce companies are enhancing their supply chains and forming strategic alliances with third-party logistics providers to fulfil the growing need for prompt and dependable delivery.
E-commerce platforms place a premium on consumer reviews and ratings, and credible brands carefully maintain their online reputations to attract new customers.

Methods for Dealing with Shifting Consumer Preferences

Data-Driven Insights: 1. Constantly collect and analyse customer data to acquire insights into shifting behaviours and preferences. You can use this data to better target your customers with your marketing efforts.

Second, use personalization tactics to provide customers what they want—including useful material, product suggestions, and promotional offers.

Thirdly, Multi-Channel Presence: Increase your online presence in locations where your target audience spends time, such as your website, social media, marketplaces, and mobile apps.

Provide prompt responses to client questions and concerns across several communication channels (live chat, email, and social media).

Fifth, Sustainability Initiatives: Integrate sustainability into your business's core values and activities, and spread the word about your commitment to environmental responsibility.

6. Subscription Services: Research subscription-based models that reward customers with ease, savings, and continued use.

7 Supply Chain Optimisation: Improve inventory management and order fulfilment times by streamlining your supply chain.

Trust from customers can be gained by openness about price, fees, and delivery charges.

Mobile Optimisation 9 Ensure a smooth mobile purchasing experience by prioritising a mobile-friendly website and app design.

Promote user-generated content like as reviews, ratings, and user-created content to increase social proof and customer trust.

Issues and Things to Think About

It can be difficult to keep up with the ways in which online shoppers' habits are shifting:

Respect the rights and privacy of your customers by collecting and using their information lawfully and ethically, as outlined in applicable data privacy rules.

2. Competition: Maintain vigilance in the face of intense rivalry by always innovating and setting yourself out from the pack.

Thirdly, Supply Chain Disruptions: Be flexible enough to adjust to changes in your supply chain, as occurred during global catastrophes like the COVID-19 epidemic.

Invest in strong cybersecurity procedures to safeguard client information and keep their trust. 4.

5. Brand Consistency: Make sure there is uniformity in the way your brand is represented and communicated to customers across all platforms.

Conclusion

Changes in technology, societal norms, and market conditions all have an impact on consumers and their habits. Successful e-commerce enterprises will anticipate these shifts, put customers first, and adjust their approaches to reflect the tastes of today's consumers. E-commerce firms may meet and even surpass the expectations of today's consumers and prosper in the dynamic digital marketplace by maintaining a focus on their customers, embracing customization, and implementing sustainable practises.

10.3- Preparing your e-commerce business for the future.

Technology, consumer preferences, and market forces all contribute to the ever-changing landscape of online shopping. E-commerce companies, in order to succeed in the present and future, need to be flexible and responsive. In this detailed manual, we'll talk about how to position your online store for future success in the face of both threats and possibilities.

Adopt new forms of technology

E-commerce relies heavily on technological innovations, therefore it's crucial to keep up of tech developments. Key technological considerations include the following:

To improve customer experiences and streamline operations, businesses can use AI-driven personalisation, chatbots for customer care, and predictive analytics.

- Augmented Reality (AR) and Virtual Reality (VR): Investigate AR and VR technologies for lifelike virtual fitting rooms and visualisations of products.

Think about blockchain for its potential uses in supply chain management and increased safety and transparency in financial dealings.

Take advantage of the increased speed and connection of 5G networks as they become more common to enhance mobile shopping experiences and real-time data processing.

Connecting smart gadgets to e-commerce platforms allows for the creation of novel product offerings and the collection of valuable customer data, both of which increase client engagement.

Secondly, Give Attention to the Customer

Online businesses depend critically on satisfied customers. Think about implementing these tactics:

- Personalization: Keep pouring money into personalization that is powered by data so that suggestions for products, content, and promotions can be made based on what customers actually want.

- User-Friendly Design: Give top priority to designing an easy-to-navigate website or app that is optimised for mobile use.

Reduce shopping cart abandonment with a streamlined checkout procedure that allows for one-click payments, guest checkouts, and several payment options.

Provide multi-channel customer service with guaranteed fast response times to questions and complaints.
To appeal to customers' increasing eco-awareness and ethical concerns, it's important to align your brand with sustainability activities.

Third, a presence on several channels.

Increase your online visibility across platforms to meet customers where they spend time:

To reach a larger audience, you may want to consider selling your wares on online marketplaces such as Amazon, eBay, or Etsy.

Use shoppable posts, stories, and influencer partnerships to generate direct sales on social media platforms; this strategy is known as "Social Commerce."

Spend money on a mobile app that's tailored specifically to the needs of mobile shoppers.

Opportunity analysis for entering foreign markets and satisfying a worldwide clientele.

Fourth, making choices based on data.

Information is a crucial resource for online stores. Put money into data analysis and the methods you use to make choices:
- Data Collection and Analysis: Constantly collect and analyse data about customers to learn more about their habits, likes, and trends.

Key performance indicators (KPIs) should be tracked on a consistent basis in order to assess the efficacy of initiatives and spot development opportunities.

- Predictive Analytics: Make use of predictive analytics to foresee patterns in client actions and demand.

5.Optimizing the Supply Chain

Timely and cost-efficient order fulfilment is dependent on excellent supply chain management:

- Inventory Management: Use optimisation strategies to keep stock levels just right, avoid stockouts, and cut down on storage fees.

Improve your fulfilment and shipping times by teaming up with a third-party logistics (3PL) company.

To accommodate the demands of environmentally conscious customers, businesses should adopt sustainable supply chain practises.

Safety in Online Transactions, No. 6
Improve safety protocols to safeguard sensitive consumer information and sustain credibility:

For cyber defence, it's important to put money into things like firewalls, encryption, and frequent audits.

Protect the privacy of your customers by adhering to data privacy standards like the General Data Protection Regulation and the California Consumer Privacy Act.

7: Maintaining Brand Integrity and Reputation

It's crucial to maintain uniformity in both brand communications and public relations efforts:

Keep your brand's message and values consistent across all of your platforms so that your customers can easily identify you.

- Online Reputation: Proactively handle ratings and reviews to increase client trust and confidence.

Sustainability Efforts, Number Eight

Consumers are becoming increasingly interested in sustainability. Think about how to include environmental considerations into your company's operations:
Reduce the environmental effect of your business by providing customers with eco-friendly and sustainable product options.

- Ethical Sourcing: Be sure that all raw materials and finished goods are sourced in a fair and honest manner.

- Circular Economy: Look into recycling and refurbishing as examples of circular economy models to cut down on waste and boost environmental friendliness.

9. Adapt to New Regulations

Maintain familiarity with the ever-changing e-commerce compliance standards. It's important to be flexible in the face of changing regulations.

10 Always Trying New Things

Create an environment where employees are encouraged to ask questions and share ideas. Motivate your staff to learn about new developments in the field, participate in training, and test out innovative approaches and technologies.

Conclusion

E-commerce future-readiness calls for a proactive strategy that embraces technology, places a premium on customer experiences, and is in tune with shifting consumer values. E-commerce enterprises may survive in and profit from today's dynamic digital market by maintaining a focus on flexibility, data, and the needs of their customers. The ability to develop and adapt will be your biggest advantage in maintaining success in e-commerce, so keep in mind that preparing for the future is a continual adventure.

www.ingramcontent.com/pod-product-compliance
Lightning Source LLC
LaVergne TN
LVHW021238080526
838199LV00088B/4572